Carlos Henrique Soares Barrozo

COMPLIANCE & SANCTIONS

Functions of Punishment in the Criminal Liability of Legal Entities

AMBRA UNIVERSITY press

Publisher: Ambra University Press
First edition: January 2026 (Revision 1.0a)

Author: Carlos Henrique Soares Barrozo.
Title: Compliance & Sanctions: Functions of Punishment in the Criminal Liability of Legal Entities
Cover design: Ambra University Press
Book design: Ambra University Press
Proofreading: Ambra University Press

E-book format: EPUB
Print format: Print format: Paperback- 6 x 9 inch

ISBN: 978-1-966958-27-7 (Print - Paperback)
ISBN: 978-1-966958-26-0 (e-book – EPUB)
Library of Congress Control Number: 2025950115

Ambra is a trademark of Ambra Education, Inc. registered in the U.S. Patent and Trademark Office.
Ambra University Press is a division of Ambra Education, Inc.
Orlando, FL, USA
https://press.ambra.education/ • https://www.ambra.education/

Editora: Ambra University Press
Primeira edição: janeiro 2026 (Revisão 1.01)

Autor: Carlos Henrique Soares Barrozo.
Título: Compliance & Sanctions: Functions of Punishment in the Criminal Liability of Legal Entities
Design da capa: Ambra University Press
Projeto gráfico: Ambra University Press
Revisão: Ambra University Press

Formato e-book: EPUB
Formato impresso: Capa mole - 6 x 9 polegadas

ISBN: 978-1-966958-27-7 (Impresso – capa mole)
ISBN: 978-1-966958-26-0 (e-book – EPUB)
Library of Congress Control Number: 2025950115

Ambra é uma marca da Ambra Education, Inc. registrada no U.S. Patent and Trademark Office.
Ambra University Press é uma divisão da Ambra Education, Inc.
Orlando, FL, EUA
https://press.ambra.education/ • https://www.ambra.education/

TABLE OF CONTENTS

ABOUT THE AUTHOR

Carlos Henrique Soares Barrozo

Carlos Henrique Soares Barrozo is an attorney specializing in Compliance, holds a Master's degree in Risk & Compliance from Ambra University (USA), and is the author of internationally recognized technical works. He has strategic experience in structuring corporate governance for international expansion and preventing legal risks. He is a member of the Brazilian Bar Association (OAB), the Compliance National Association, and the Ibero-American Institute of Compliance, and has been awarded for excellence in compliance and governance. Barrozo has published articles in peer-reviewed journals and is the author of a national bill on corporate compliance, combining practice, research, and innovation in the legal field.

INTRODUCTION

During the year 1940, the Penal Code (CP) was promulgated, which came into force in that year. In this scenario, the criminal liability of the business entity was not effectively addressed by jurists and legislators. This is because it is known that the primary objective of the punitive law was to criminally penalize only individuals. Thus, when it comes to the business entity, a context of invisibility was still observed, that is, for the sanctioning law, the company[1] had no value for the purposes of liability (Brazil, 1940).

It so happens that, in 1988, there was the promulgation of the current Federal Constitution (FC), with provisions that carry the possibility of an effective accountability of the business entity. Although the Constitutional Text ensures the aforementioned possibility of punishment, the ordinary legislator did not consider that, when analyzing the legal concepts that support criminal punishment, e.g., the concept of conduct, culpability and the function of the penalty, punitive legislation would not be perfectly adequate for such conviction (Federal Constitution, 1988).

In this sense, it is worth mentioning that the concepts addressed have been the target of criticism by the doctrine, as exposed by the jurist and magistrate

---

1 In the present work, the concept of "company" adopted is similar to the concept of business entity, distancing itself from the concept established by business law. While the latter defines "company" as the exercise of "organized economic activity for the production or circulation of goods or services", as provided for by Article 966 of the Civil Code (Brazil, 2002, p. 70), the approach in this dissertation will consider the "company" as an entity distinct from its partners or managers and endowed with its own legal personality, capable of acting in the market and assuming obligations and rights.

Zaffaroni when he states that some criminal rules were created exclusively aiming at a sentence against the individual, disregarding the application of the aforementioned concepts for the purpose of imposing penalties on companies (Zaffaroni, 1997, p. 390).

However, it is important to mention that in Brazil the criminal liability of the business entity is indeed a reality, with regard to the trial for environmental crimes, being supported by Law No. 9,605/98. This legal framework not only confirms the feasibility of punishing the corporate entity, but also meets the constitutional mandate of environmental protection (Brazil, 1998).

In view of this, it is also possible to consider the role of the functions of punishment in terms of criminal liability, which were created to justify the existence of criminal sentences in the face, at least in principle, of individuals. However, the purposes of the penalty, when analyzed in depth, would not be adequate to properly justify the condemnation of the companies or, at least, would not be applied in a proportional manner when individuals are taken as a parameter.

It is clarified that the functions of the penalty aim to prevent future criminal practices and to repay the crime committed with a punishment proportional to the offense. Regarding the preventive purpose, in a very brief way, it seeks to persuade society and the offender to refrain from committing future criminal acts. In fact, persuasion often occurs through the effective fulfillment of prison sentences. Therefore, it has a great role linked to the cognitive sphere of people, that is, it refers to the set of mental processes and activities related to the knowledge and perception of the human mind. In addition, this purpose requires the effective fulfillment of serious punishments in the criminal sphere, so that the fear of criminal consequences, the neutralization of the individual and other characteristics can be generated.

Regarding the function of retribution of the penalty, there is truly a disproportion between the damage caused and the impact that there will be on the company, in response to the act committed. This analysis starts, as will be appreciated throughout the work, from the perspective that individuals, when they are punished, face very serious punishments in response to the acts, having to sacrifice years of life to compensate for the criminal act. However, when analyzing the punishments of business entities are mild, not genuinely generating a proportionality corresponding to the damage caused, which requires an analysis of such a situation.

Thus, the theme addressed in the present work is justified by covering a significant legal and social context. Thus, the damages related to the corporation, especially with regard to the twenty-first century, increase the relevance of the criminal liability of this agent, since critical injuries to essential legal assets are generated by large companies.

These challenges can be considered contemporary in the criminal sphere, since many corporate crimes neglect the due consideration of responsibility, based on the purposes of punishment, focusing predominantly on that of the individual who represents it. The research aims to fill this gap, contributing to a more comprehensive and critical understanding of the capacity of legal entities to be criminally punished in attention to the purposes of the sanction.

Appropriately, as mentioned by the judge of the Court of Justice of Rio Grande do Sul, Eladio Lecey, the most serious injuries to the environment are predominantly caused by business entities. In fact, such damages not only impact the personal interests of specific individuals or social groups, but also put at risk fundamental legal assets, such as the preservation of life for present and future generations (Lecey, 1999, p. 171).

It can be noted that there are theoretical and practical challenges that are linked to this theme. One of the challenges to be faced concerns the principle of the personality of the penalty, which is linked to the function of the sanction provided for in the criminal code, not allowing, in general, that the penalty has effects beyond the person of the convicted. Another challenge that deserves to be highlighted is that of the theory of double imputation, a topic that has already been considered in the higher courts, which addresses the need or not for the presence of individuals together with the legal entity in a possible sentence against the latter.

It should also be noted that the extent of the losses caused by a business entity, when briefly contrasted with that caused by an individual, has the considerable potential to cause damages of significant magnitude to the community, including those of an irreversible nature. In this context, the retributive function of punishment emerges, whose purpose is to compel the agent to face the consequences of the harm perpetrated by it, in line with the notion of fair consideration.

Consequently, the judiciary, bound by statutory rules, is limited to the quantum of the penalty to which the business entity would be bound, which, as will be seen, is far below the damage caused to society, contrary to the functions of the penalty. Thus, it deserves a readjustment of the aforementioned purpose aiming at the correct application of the penalty in the specific case.

Therefore, considering the justification mentioned for this dissertation, it should be said that it has as its object of research the criminal liability of the business entity, focusing specifically on the functions of each penalty that can be applied to society. The central problem lies in the adequacy of the purposes of each sanction, which have traditionally been designed for the accountability of individuals, in the context of corporate entities.

Regarding the methodology, it will be conducted through an extensive bibliographic review, adopting a critical approach, with doctrinal and jurisprudential analysis, aiming to identify gaps and inconsistencies in the application of the purposes of the penalty to the business entity. Case studies will also be used to exemplify how judicial decisions have interpreted and applied the current norms in the Brazilian scenario. It should be mentioned that there will be a qualitative approach, by extensively examining relevant cases of corporate damages punished in the criminal sphere, promoting a dialogue between the theory and the legal practice of the purposes of punishment.

Having overcome the aforementioned issues, the present work will address the "Theoretical Foundation and the Criminal Liability of the Business Entity", exploring the legal and doctrinal foundations that support the possibility and challenges of criminal liability of corporate entities in Brazil. Primarily, the application of the "Functions of Punishment and the Relationship with the Business Entity" will be discussed, examining how the preventive and retributive purposes of the penalty are or are not adequate to the punishment of collective entities. Finally, the jurisprudence of the Supreme Courts and the International Court will be addressed, comparing experiences from other legal systems and investigating paradigmatic judicial decisions that influence the interpretation and application of criminal liability, contributing to a critical and contextualized analysis of the theoretical and practical challenges faced in this field of law.

The research will thus seek to contribute to a critical analysis of the functions of punishment in this specific context, providing valuable insights into the implications on the fundamental principles of criminal law. Thus, the choice of the theme is justified by the ability to promote a deeper and more grounded understanding of the capacity and limitations of criminal liability of corporate entities, promoting an essential debate for the improvement of the Brazilian justice system in this specific area of law, that is, the purposes of punishment.

THEORETICAL FOUNDATIONS AND THE CRIMINAL LIABILITY OF THE BUSINESS ENTITY

This chapter on "theoretical foundation and the criminal liability of the busines entity" is intended to analyze the theories of the company, that is, guidelines that base the recognition of the corporate entity by law. In this way, it is mentioned that there are two bases that exist, that of Fiction and that of Reality.

Once the company's legal basis is overcome, all the ways in which the corporate entity can be punished, which are dealt with by the Citizen Constitution, will be assessed[2]. Therefore, article 173, § 5 and article 225, § 3, which refers to the Environmental Criminal Liability Law (Law 9.605/1998), will be analyzed.

Finally, there will be an analysis of the limitations and compatibility in the criminal liability of the business entity. In the meantime, some prerequisites for the feasibility of condemning the company in the criminal sphere will be

---

2 The Federal Constitution of 1988 is recognized as a "Citizen Constitution" for its inclusive and democratic aspect, significantly expanding social rights by recognizing rights such as health, education, decent work and social security. In addition, it strengthened individual and collective guarantees, consolidated democratic principles, such as universal suffrage and the separation of powers, and sought environmental protection and sustainable development (Federal Constitution, 1988).

demonstrated, which were established by the doctrine, as explained below, and are often followed by the main national courts.

On the subject of limitations on liability, it is necessary to examine the Principle of Personality of the Penalty, which stipulates that the effects of the sentence will fall on the one who committed the criminal conduct. In this context, it is noteworthy that certain minority shareholders are affected by decisions that have repercussions in the criminal sphere by the majority shareholders, even if they have abstained or voted against it in business resolutions. It will be demonstrated that, also according to the aforementioned principle, corporate transactions involving the reorganization of companies generate the extinction of punishment in criminal law, which eliminates any possibility of applying the functions of the penalty, even if there is practical continuity of the business entity.

Finally, it will be highlighted, there will be a joint analysis of the speed of the statute of limitations for environmental crimes and the complexity of the great damages caused by companies that require time, resources and people to carry out the entire procedural process.

THEORIES OF THE BUSINESS ENTITY

In order to be able to examine precisely what the criminal liability of the business entity consists of, it is necessary to analyze the theoretical foundation, that is, the legal nature, of the former. In this way, analyzing the essence of the corporate entity in the eyes of the national law, it becomes possible to make a certain capacity for criminal punishment feasible or unfeasible for actions manifested by collective entities.

In view of this, this chapter aims to present the theories brought by jurists who deal with this subject, which are recognized by the higher courts, which justify the legal nature of the corporate entity, thus seeking to understand the limitations in acquiring rights and contracting obligations, as well as having the capacity to respond to a possible criminal process.

In this scenario, two major guidelines, discussed later, have enormous space, being widely recognized by the doctrine that studies corporate law and with application by the major courts of the country. The first of them is called Theory of Fiction, which was developed by Friedrich Carl von Savigny, one of the main German jurists of the nineteenth century, while the second basis is mentioned as Theory of Reality, announced by Hugo Grotius, a Dutch jurist and founder of international law (Savigny, 1879; Grocio, 2005).

Theory of Fiction

At the outset, on the subject of the theory of fiction, it is essential to bring certain comments from its main defender, Savigny (Savigny, 1879). According to the aforementioned jurist, the legal personality would not have any real existence to be considered, it would only be a construction created by jurists. Therefore, this basis is centered on the idea that only the individual can hold rights.

Thus, such arguments are considered extremely limited in terms of the rights conferred on companies, since existence was conditioned to only facilitate certain functions of individuals. Therefore, the purpose of its existence was to facilitate legal and institutional relations between individuals.

In this scenario, it is worth mentioning that the existence of the so-called theory of fiction is based on the idea that any company should be seen as a fiction created by law, having only a merely legal existence. In this context, in the factual world, business entities would not have any capacity for action, and as a consequence, they could not be targets of possible criminal liability.

Thus, the professor of criminal law at the Faculty of Law of UFMG, Sheila Sales, points out (Sales, 1993, p. 29), that "business entities are fictitious entities, created by the Law, having their own consciousness and will, that is, the psychic conditions capable of determining the will". In addition, it adds that "they do not have, therefore, the capacity to act and, consequently, are not subject to punishment in the criminal sphere, since the assumptions on which the modern Criminal Law of guilt is based are absent".

In this sense, it is extracted from this theory the unfeasibility of any criminal liability on the part of the business entity, since it would lack the capacity to conduct and the possibility of culpability. It is interesting to mention that part of the Brazilian doctrine, by stating that the company does not have criminal capacity, tends to affiliate with this guideline, according to the jurist and magistrate Eugenio Raúl Zaffaroni, the prosecutor Julio Fabbrini Mirabete, the jurist Rogério Greco, among others, who state that they do not have the possibility of practicing conducts, in the manner outlined by the code, thus preventing imputability (Zaffaroni, 1996, p. 339; Greco, 2007, p. 173; Mirabete, 2004, p. 122).

Consequently, any action taken by a company that offends a criminally protected legal asset, it would be up to the public power to sue the individuals who manage, direct and carry out activities, since it would be these, for the theory of fiction, who would have committed the alleged crime. It is added that criminal law would have a punitive function only for individuals, excluding all corporate entities (Shecaira, 1998, p. 86).

In fact, according to the jurist who defends the theory of fiction, Vareilles-Sommières, the business entity is incapable of committing small faults or infractions. The responsibility for failures and violations falls exclusively on individuals, that is, the partners and representatives who embody the spirit of society (Vareilles-Sommieres, 1919).

An issue that deserves to be highlighted, regarding the theory of fiction, concerns the agent's responsibility, which can be objective or subjective. In the Civil Code (CC), it was prescribed in article 927, sole paragraph, that "There will be an obligation to repair the damage, regardless of fault, in the cases specified by law, or when the activity normally carried out by the author of the damage implies, by its nature, a risk to the rights of others" (Brazil, 2002, p. 67). In this way, in light of the CC, a civil punishment of the business entity would be perfectly appropriate, since no guilt or even any conduct would be discussed, there would be a duty to indemnify.

On the other hand, when analyzing criminal law, especially article 18, sole paragraph, it is said that "Except in the cases expressed by law, no one can be punished for a fact foreseen as a crime, except when he commits it intentionally" (Brazil, 1940, p. 4). Therefore, the rule of the Penal Code (CP) is inverse to that of the CC, where there would be a need for guilt of the agent for the imputation of the crime to this guideline. However, the Theory of fiction further develops all the punitive legislation, since, in order to be addressing a subject of culpability, a certain conduct of the agent would be implicit, which would also not be accepted by this current.

Thus, in order for there to be criminal liability, it would be required that the active subject of the criminal offense be an individual, and it cannot be a company, since this would be a fiction of law. Thus, it can be mentioned that, for this theory, the action of the corporate entity would be impaired since it could never carry out a conduct without an individual representing it.

However, it is known that punitive legislation is not closed solely to the subjective responsibility of the agent who commits crimes, because, as the Judge, Doctor of Criminal Law Thiago De Filippo, teaches, there are cases of objective criminal punishment, such as in the crimes of theft and reception, and in special causes of penalty increase, therefore, This is what the author says:

> However, we cannot deny the existence of remnants of strict criminal liability in our system. Two examples from the jurisprudence are symptomatic. The first of them consists of the inversion of the proof of intent in some crimes against property, such as theft and reception. If the subject is found in the possession of the defendant, it is up to him to prove his non-guilt, thus admitting the improper subjective responsibility in Criminal Law.
>
> The second is the hypothesis of the incidence of special causes of increase, regardless of proof that the agent was aware of this circumstance. Specifically, in the case of drug trafficking practiced

> on the premises or in the vicinity of schools, hospitals, etc., mere geographical proximity is sufficient, ignoring the evidence that the agent knew or should have known about this circumstance, which is a clear example of strict criminal liability as to the aggravation of the sanction (De Filippo, 2016, p. 3).

Despite all the points mentioned, the theory that denies that the legal entity is merely a fiction, as Savigny maintained, prevails in modern times. In this sense, it is currently widely accepted that the company is a reality and that it differs substantially from the reality of individuals (Savigny, 1879).

Theory of Reality

The second guideline on the theoretical foundation of the legal entity is the theory of reality or objective, organic reality or real will or personality. This, in fact, is the most accepted strand in Brazilian jurisprudence and doctrine, as shown in the text below.

The theory of reality consists of attributing its own personality to the business entity, regardless of the members, partners, shareholders, making it seen as an autonomous entity endowed with its own will, whose purpose is the achievement of the social purpose.

This theory had as its precursor the aforementioned jurist Hugo Grócio, who always equated the business entity with the individual, arguing that not only the individual, but also the corporate entity, would be endowed with real existence and capable of being the subject of rights and, consequently, of duties, and could have a triple responsibility, administrative, civil and criminal (Grócio, 2005).

It is worth mentioning that, because there is its own will, for this theory, the business entity could be held criminally responsible for the commission of crimes. This is due to the fact that, through one's own will, it would be possible to direct the activities to the practice of crimes.

It should be clarified that such a perspective is consistent with the Brazilian Constitutional Text, which prescribes, in fact, the criminal liability of the company in certain cases, which will be discussed later.

In order to provide a practical basis on the application of the theory of reality in the higher courts, it is mentioned that the Supreme Court of Justice (STJ), when deciding on the matter of a Regimental Appeal in the Special Appeal, asserts that there is indeed the possibility of criminal liability of the business entity, as defended by the theory of reality. In the judgment in question, although the discussion was related to the statute of limitations, the feasibility of criminal conviction of the company was clearly clear[3].

According to the important German jurist, Otto von Gierke, the persona moralis (company) has a body endowed with a special personality that remains unchanged, even if the members (natural persons) change. For the author, the business entity's capacity for action would be instituted by a supreme authority. In this way, in each and every corporate entity there would be an empire and independence of the body over the members (Gierke, 1934).

It is also essential to cite the lessons of Sérgio Salomão Shecaira, professor, master and doctor in criminal law, who clarifies that the business entity is not a fantasy, since it is "concretized at each important stage of its life by the meeting, deliberation and vote of the general assembly of its members, or even through its administration or management" (Shecaira, 1998, p. 88).

---

3 "AGRG IN RESP 1712991 / SP 2017/0313343-9." "CRIMINAL. INTERLOCUTORY APPEAL IN THE SPECIAL APPEAL. ENVIRONMENTAL CRIME. LEGAL ENTITY. STATUTE OF LIMITATIONS. COUNT. TERM OF CUSTODIAL SENTENCES. PRESCRIPTION. NON-OCCURRENCE. PREVIOUS. APPEAL DISMISSED. 1. In environmental crimes, although the imposition of custodial sentences on legal entities is inapplicable, the statute of limitations must comply with the rule of article 109, sole paragraph, of the CP, which establishes that the same deadlines defined for the prescription of corporal punishment are applicable to sanctions restricting rights. 2. Regimental appeal dismissed". "Rapporteur: Minister Nefi Cordeiro" (Brazil, 1940, p. 20; Supreme Court of Justice, 2018, p. 1).

Finally, regarding the theory of reality, which brings the possibility of holding business entities criminally liable, it should be pointed out that there may be different thoughts alleging that, even in the face of the aforementioned theory, the principle of societas delinquere non potest should be considered, which means that the corporate entity cannot commit crimes or be able to be punished by the criminal sphere. However, it must be recognized that the Federal Constitution itself brings such a provision, which will be discussed later, which leads to believe that the aforementioned legal basis would not have a current application.

In view of this, it is necessary to analyze, in the light of the FC, how the criminal liability of the business entity would be affirmed in the Brazilian legal system.

CONSTITUTION AND CRIMINAL LIABILITY OF THE BUSINESS ENTITY

The criminal liability of the business entity, despite being seen as something unprecedented in the Brazilian scenario, has already been a reality in the Brazilian empire, remaining after that for decades without space in any legislative field in the country. Notwithstanding this fact, the national panorama came to be changed with the new Federal Constitution (Brazil, 1988).

It is worth mentioning that, according to the Prosecutor and internationally renowned specialist in Economic Criminal Law Paulo César Busato, "the impulse to arrive at ordinary legislation and even the Penal Code with the theme of the RPPJ came from a legitimate constitutional initiative". In fact, the author adds that the FC, "which clearly has a profile of defense of individual guarantees to the point of being called a citizen Constitution" (Busato, 2018, p. 91).

Today, all the guidelines for criminal liability of the legal entity are found in the Federal Constitution. This delimits which branches of law can be dealt with by the legislator for the typification of a certain conduct, carried out by the company.

It so happens that the provisions present in the Federal Constitution are presented as constitutional norms of limited effectiveness, that is, it is not possible for society to use such norms to produce the rights now affirmed therein, so that they have effects in factual scenarios. Thus, any constitutional provision without the proper law, ordinary or complementary, that disciplines it, makes the aforementioned constitutional provisions unenforceable.

Therefore, it is necessary to emphasize that the Constitution of the Republic of Brazil truly presents itself as a Citizen Constitution, this is due to the fact that it shows a progressive and inclusive character. In addition, it brought in its provisions the protection of social, economic, cultural and environmental rights. Therefore, it is noticeable that the constitutional text was conceived with citizenship and the protection of fundamental rights in mind, reinforcing democratic and social values.

From this scenario, there was the possibility of the existence of the liability of the legal entity beyond the civil and administrative spheres, because it encompassed the criminal sphere. It is worth mentioning that the CF has become of great importance in this new form of condemnation, bringing unique provisions that allow the punishment of the company in various acts, namely, those practiced against the economic order, the financial, the popular economy and the environment.

Analysis of Article 173, § 5

With the emergence of the so-called corporate criminality, a situation that is expanding in post-modern and contemporary society, numerous legal thinkers have been concerned with such a situation, this is because the complexity and dimension of crimes are far beyond what any individual alone could practice. It is mentioned that this criminality of the business entity involves an accentuated risk, since due to its economic performance in the market, it may be faced with a capacity to irreparably reach several regions or by the structure itself, to cover up new crimes committed by the business entity (Botelho, 2004, p. 228).

Regarding the new form of condemnation of the company, the Federal Constitution played a fundamental role in this situation. Before the existence of the constitutional provisions that deal with the subject, discussed below, it was inconceivable to believe that the Penal Code of 1940 could allow a business entity to be at the passive pole of a criminal proceeding.

In this sense, the first constitutional provision to be analyzed refers to article 173, paragraph 5, of the Federal Constitution, which asserts that the law will establish the liability of the business entity, according to the punishments compatible with the legal nature, in cases of crimes against the economic, financial and popular economy.[4]

Therefore, the aforementioned constitutional provision opens doors to a criminal liability of the business entity, in addition to that referring to the company's directors. It is also worth mentioning that the practices that a certain business entity could carry out, which would be understood as criminal types, would only be those practiced against the economic, financial and popular economy order.

Despite the clarity of the constitutional text, part of the doctrine – explained below – understands that punishments compatible with the legal nature of the corporate entity, when they are involved in transgressions of the economic, financial and popular economy, would not include criminal liability, as

---

4 "Article 173. Except for the cases provided for in this Constitution, the direct exploitation of economic activity by the State will only be allowed when necessary for the imperatives of national security or for the relevant collective interest, as defined by law" (Federal Constitution, 1988, p. 112). Article 173, § 5: "The law, without prejudice to the individual responsibility of the directors of the business entity, shall establish the liability of the latter, subjecting it to punishments compatible with its nature, in acts practiced against the economic and financial order and against the popular economy" (Federal Constitution, 1988, p. 112).

defended, for example, by Professor René Ariel Dotti, who mentions that crimes or misdemeanors and misdemeanors cannot be committed by companies, in the same way, says Dr. Duek Marques, who mentions that collective entities can only assign civil or administrative sanctions. This is due to the fact that the Federal Constitution has omitted to exhaustively mention each area of law in which the business entity could be the target of a certain punishment (Dotti, 1995, p. 201; Marques, 1998, p. 7).

In fact, the provision that was contained in the draft of the 1988 Constitution is raised by many, which left no doubt about the new way for the company to be criminally sanctioned, if it were the case of a transgression of this nature. The provision would once be worded as follows, which would correspond to the current article 173 of the Federal Constitution: "Article 202. Paragraph 5 - The law, without prejudice to the individual responsibility of the members of the legal entity, shall establish the criminal liability of the latter, subjecting it to penalties compatible with its nature, in crimes committed against the economic and financial order and the popular economy" (Federal Constitution, 1988, p. 112).

It can be seen that there were two changes that occurred through the intervention of the Systematization Commission, in 1987. The first of these was the suppression of the word "criminal" and the second with the change of the word "crimes" to "acts". This ended up dividing the opinions of jurists, as exposed, where some assure that the criminal liability of the business entity would not be a reality in Brazil and others understand that the constitutional legislator sought not to delimit the area of the corporation's capacity to be punished, but to allow it to be as broad as possible, according to the doctrinaires mentioned above.

It turns out that the criminal laws that typify various crimes against the financial and economic order, including against the popular economy, did not address the criminal liability of the company, bringing, in their core, provisions that condemn the practice of certain conducts of the individual. Therefore, conduct practiced by business entities, which despite having a certain correspondent when it comes to individuals, are not judged when these practices are materialized by a corporate entity, due to the absence of legal provision.

Finally, it is worth mentioning that the laws that deal with criminal acts committed against the economic, financial and popular economy order, namely, laws 8,078/1990, 8,137/1990 and 8,176/1991, did not materialize the criminal liability of the business entity (Brodt and Meneghin, 2015).

It should also be said that, in light of article 173, paragraph 5, of the Federal Constitution, money laundering, which aims to hide or disguise the illicit origin of values, could potentially fit into that context, especially considering the need to protect the economic and financial order against criminal activities.

In this sense, it is worth making considerations about the OECD, which is the Organization for Economic Cooperation and Development, promoting economic policies to improve the economic and social well-being of member and non-member countries. It develops standards and guidelines in various areas, including economics, tax policy, trade, and the environment.

Based on this scenario, the OECD held the Convention against Corruption, which was ratified by Brazil, its importance materializes in the global aspect, since it is a problem that affects the economic development of countries. The Convention aims to prevent and combat bribery of foreign public officials in international business transactions. In addition, it explicitly defines and criminalizes bribery of foreign public officials, establishing that signatory countries must adjust their legislation to effectively combat this corrupt practice (OECD, 2016).

In addition to criminalizing natural persons involved in the bribery of foreign public officials, the Convention also makes room, in Article 2, for the accountability of business entities linked to these acts of transnational corruption. Therefore, companies that participate in corrupt practices, according to article 3 of the convention, should be punished with effective, proportional and dissuasive criminal penalties, similar to those applied to domestic corruption (OECD, 2016, p. 11).

In addition, the FATF, Financial Action Task Force, which was created within the OECD, also acts against money laundering, this is an intergovernmental group established to develop and promote policies to combat this crime and the financing of terrorism globally. The FATF establishes the International Recommendations on Combating Money Laundering and the Financing of Terrorism and Proliferation, which are widely adopted by countries around the world as international standards (FATF, 2012).

For the present topic, FATF Recommendation 3 is especially relevant, as it deals with the obligation of countries to criminalize money laundering based on the United Nations Conventions against Illicit Traffic in Drugs and Psychotropic Substances (Vienna Convention, 2009) and against Transnational Organized Crime (Palermo Convention, 2004). The recommendation states that countries should apply the crime of money laundering to all serious offences, with a view to including a wide range of antecedent crimes, whether they are described by categories, minimum penalties or lists of specific crimes (FATF, 2012, p. 14).

In addition, the Interpretative Note emphasizes the importance of holding business entities accountable for involvement in money laundering activities, providing that, when criminal liability is not possible due to fundamental principles of national law, civil or administrative sanctions must be applied. These measures ensure that business entities are effectively punished, regardless of the form of accountability adopted, and allow the coexistence of parallel criminal, civil or administrative proceedings, when allowed by the country's legal system. All sanctions should be effective, proportionate, and dissuasive, ensuring that punishment is adequate to prevent and combat the practice of money laundering, without prejudice to the criminal accountability of individuals involved (The FATF Recommendations, 2023, p. 39).

In view of the above, the implementation of international policies and guidelines, such as those promoted by the OECD and the FATF, are crucial for mitigating the risks associated with money laundering. This is an essential tool to strengthen countries' capacity to identify and correct deviations challenged by regulations, thus promoting the integrity of global financial systems.

It is worth noting that, although the FATF states that these recommendations constitute "soft law", as they are not mandatory, it paradoxically expects all countries to accept and implement them, raising the question of whether these Recommendations are not, in fact, a form of "hard law", as stated by the jurist Alberico Mendonça (Mendonça, 2007).

In the case of the United Nations, it should be noted that Brazil ratified, by Decree 154, of June 26, 1991, the United Nations Convention against Illicit Traffic in Narcotic Drugs and Psychotropic Substances, known as the Vienna Convention. It should be mentioned that Article 3 of the Convention states that countries must criminalize as a crime in their domestic legislation the conversion or transfer of assets knowing that they are the result of specific crimes, in addition to hiding their illegal origin or helping those involved to escape legal consequences. This is aimed at combating money laundering and other international criminal activities (Brazil, 1991, p. 3-5).

Furthermore, through Decree No. 5,015 of March 15, 2004, Brazil enacted the United Nations Convention against Transnational Organized Crime, known as the Palermo Convention, which brought light to the issue that has had a substantial increase in cases. The Convention addresses various forms of crime, including money laundering and corruption, promoting international cooperation and preventive measures to address these illicit activities on a global scale (Brazil, 2004).

In addition, Article 10 of the Convention establishes that each State Party must adopt measures to hold legal entities involved in serious offenses related to organized criminal groups accountable, which may be of a criminal, civil or administrative nature, which does not interfere with the accountability of the natural persons involved in the action. It should be added that punishments must be effective, proportional and dissuasive (Brazil, 2004, p. 5).

Thus, it has been noted that it is crucial to combat international crime, addressing money laundering, corruption and other forms of organized crime, and each government must hold business entities involved in these serious offenses accountable, both in the civil and administrative spheres, as well as in the criminal sphere. In this way, there would be effective deterrence and punishment of illicit activities on a global scale.

It is also worth mentioning the United Nations Convention against Corruption, known as the Merida Convention, ratified by Brazil through Decree No. 5,687, of January 31, 2006, representing an essential instrument in the fight against corruption. This convention also establishes measures to hold legal entities involved in acts of corruption accountable, ensuring that they are subject to effective and dissuasive punishments (Brazil, 2006).

In this context, it is vital to mention that the importance of accountability for the aforementioned crimes is not limited to the theoretical level, because practical examples such as the case of Odebrecht demonstrate its concrete relevance and global impact, or even the case of Lojas Americanas, which, despite not having international repercussions, was considered the biggest scandal of Brazilian breakdown and fraud.

In this sense, the well-known case of corruption of Odebrecht at an international level, due to the extension of its operations in several countries, especially in Latin America. Odebrecht is recognized as one of the largest contractors in Brazil and was involved in systemic corruption practices that were revealed through Operation Car Wash. She even admitted to having paid bribes in exchange for large public infrastructure contracts financed by governments, in exchange for advantages in contracts to the detriment of competitors, in several countries, including Brazil, Peru, Colombia, Venezuela, the Dominican Republic and others (Desidério, 2018).

Therefore, due to its scale and the involvement of influential politicians and businessmen in several countries, the Odebrecht scandal has become an international case. Cooperation between authorities from different nations was crucial in investigating and prosecuting those involved, reflecting the global dimension of the corporate corruption problem.

This scandal has further highlighted the importance of international conventions, such as the one promoted by the OECD and the FATF, which seek to combat corruption of foreign public officials in international business transactions and money laundering. These conventions not only establish global standards for the prevention and punishment of corruption, but also provide for the accountability not only of natural persons, but also of business entities involved in corrupt acts.

The United Nations Organization against organized crime and money laundering is also vital, seeking to combat illicit activities that transcend borders. In the context of Odebrecht, both the individuals responsible for the bribes and the company itself have been the target of investigations and sanctions in several countries.

Another case of great repercussion was that of Lojas Americanas, in 2023, through an elaborate accounting fraud, carried out over more than a decade by the company's former board of directors. It should be noted that in this scheme, there was the manipulation of financial records through practices such as the entry of fictitious expenses, recording of unrealized revenues and manipulation of assets and liabilities. This artificially increased the company's results, deceiving investors, banks and suppliers. This situation generated approximately R$ 43 billion in accounting inconsistencies, leading to a drastic drop in market value and resulting in a judicial reorganization process (Bolzani, 2023).

From this it is extracted that fraud and corruption are themes that permeate various sectors of contemporary society, from the corporate environment to the political and governmental sphere. These situations not only compromise the integrity and transparency of institutions, but also undermine public trust and negatively affect socio-economic development.

In the case of money laundering, Law No. 9,613/1998, which provides for the crimes of laundering or concealment of assets, rights and values, does not expressly provide for the criminal liability of business entities, thus lacking agreement with the rules ratified by the Federative Republic of Brazil on the FATF regulations, specifically number 3. However, the administrative and civil liability of companies involved in money laundering crimes can be applied based on other legislation, such as the Anti-Corruption Law (Law No.

12,846/2013), which allows the liability of business entities for harmful acts against the public administration, national or foreign (Law 9,613, 1998, p. 3, 5).

Therefore, money laundering crimes significantly affect the economic structure and trust in financial transactions, since this practice has the potential to destabilize markets, divert resources from lawful activities, and foster crime.

It so happens that, for all the above, due to the absence of a specific internalized law that includes the criminal liability of legal entities in the crime of money laundering, considering that, for example, the FATF recommendations have not yet been internalized for national legislation to cover business entities, this prevents their criminal liability, generating only repercussions in the administrative and civil spheres. Thus, there is a need for specific infra-constitutional legislation at the domestic level legitimizing and detailing the requirements and procedures for imputing criminal liability to legal entities in cases of corruption or money laundering, in line with the constitutional principles of legality and due process.

Finally, the theme of money laundering and corruption is reinforced, with which Maria Cordeiro, a master in law, asserts that, although the current legislation in Brazil prioritizes administrative liability, the expansion to the sphere of Criminal Law would present itself as an effective tool to contain these crimes, harmonizing the sanctioning mechanisms with the seriousness of the acts perpetrated (Cordeiro, 2023, p. 143-152).

In this sense, mention should be made of the jurist Odilon Júnior, who mentions in his studies that, despite the recommendation that there are internal rules of the FATF, "there is, however, no criminal sanction provided for business entities that practice the crime of money laundering, even though the social reproach of such crimes and the immense harmful consequences resulting from them demand the need for effective criminal punishment, not only of individuals, as already provided for by law, but also of business entities, until then subject only to the aforementioned administrative sanctions" (Júnior, 2019, p. 36).

Therefore, it is imperative that the Brazilian legislator internalize the recommendations of the FATF, which were mentioned above, so that there is a reconciliation of the responsibility of corporations with the constitutional principles of legality, proportionality and due process, ensuring a fair and equitable application of the law in the fight against money laundering and other economic crimes.

Article 173, § 5, of the Federal Constitution was not the only one that brought provisions in the sense of the criminal conviction of the legal entity, another also deals with the same theme, that is, article 225, § 3, of the Federal Constitution, which will be dealt with below.

Study of Article 225, § 3 and Environmental Criminal Liability

As for the criminal liability of the business entity for damage to the environment, the constituent legislator expressed itself more clearly, concretized in article 225, § 3, of the Federal Constitution. In this sense, the constitutional text states that crimes against the environment will subject the offender, even if they are companies, to criminal and administrative sanctions, regardless of the obligation to repair the damage caused.[5]

In this sense, when it comes to the criminal liability of business entities in environmental matters, the constitutional legislator has ensured such a possibility. This is because, regardless of the civil reparation for the damage

---

5 "Article 225. Everyone has the right to an ecologically balanced environment, a good for the common use of the people and essential to a healthy quality of life, imposing on the Government and the community the duty to defend and preserve it for present and future generations" (Federal Constitution, 1988, p. 136). Article 225, § 3: "Conducts and activities considered harmful to the environment shall subject the offenders, individuals or legal entities, to criminal and administrative sanctions, regardless of the obligation to repair the damage caused" (Federal Constitution, 1988, p. 137).

caused, nothing would take away the company's ability to be punished, resulting from the same fact, in criminal and administrative matters.

It is interesting to mention that, even with the assertiveness of the constitutional text, there is some divergence in the doctrine, as will be exposed, about the real possibility of punishing a company in the criminal sphere. The doctrinaires who defend the possibility of conviction emphasize that the "criminal and administrative sanctions" would be incident to both individual and legal offenders, without any distinction.

In this sense, for a minority portion of the doctrine, according to the jurist Miguel Reale Júnior, the constitutional provision should be interpreted in a teleological way, with a different interpretation of the real possibility of criminal coordination of the company, because, when the conditional text mentions that "they will subject the offenders, individuals or legal entities, to criminal and administrative sanctions", Individuals would be linked to punishments, however, societies would be tied only to penalties correlated to the administrative sphere. In view of this, the first sanctioning measures would be applicable to individuals and the second to corporate entities (Reale Júnior, 2001, p. 137-139).

According to the jurist Sávio Bittencourt Silva, the resistance presented by part of the doctrine would actually be a fear of change, in the words of the author, there would be a "fear of the new", as occurred with the emergence of the finalist theory of action, which had enormous resistance in its application (Silva, 2002, p. 178).

Despite the above, the ordinary legislator ended up putting an end to the doctrinal clash, when it enacted Law 9.605/1998, which involves crimes for environmental activities, demonstrating that there is, in fact, legitimacy in the criminal liability of the legal entity.

In this way, Law 9.605/1998 exposed this new form of condemnation based on two essential provisions, namely, article 3, header, and article 21, which mention that, in fact, the company will be held liable in the criminal, civil and administrative spheres for damage to the environment, provided that the violation occurs by resolution of its legal representative, or collegiate body, in favor of the interests or benefits of the corporate entity itself. In fact, the Environmental Crimes Law establishes that there are three penalties applicable to business entities, namely, fines, restrictions of rights and provision of services to the community.[6]

Therefore, through the aforementioned law, the criminal liability of the company was born, when the criminal practice is "committed by decision of its legal or contractual representative, or of its collegiate body, in the interest or benefit of its entity" and, in addition, article 21 mentions the sanctions compatible with the legal nature of the business entity, which are: fines; restrictive rights; and provision of services to the community (Brazil, 1998, p. 1, 3).

It is interesting to mention the position of the German jurist, Roxin, who asserts that "sanctions against business entities will play a great role in the future. After all, the most socially harmful forms of economic and environmental crime originate in large and powerful companies; also the sale of the most diverse products harmful to health will be an increasing problem for Criminal Law". It is added that not only would there be the aforementioned significant harm in environmental crimes, but also the practices of money laundering and the use of business entities to apply fraud and scams generate a tremendous shock in society (Roxin, 2013, p. 27).

In this sense, it is mentioned that the harmful potential that an individual has in relation to the environment is often lower than the harmful potential that a company has. These can cause several large-scale damages to the environment,

---

6 "Article 3 Legal entities shall be held administratively, civilly and criminally liable in accordance with the provisions of this Law, in cases where the infraction is committed by decision of their legal or contractual representative, or of their collegiate body, in the interest or benefit of their entity" (Brazil, 1998, p. 1). "Article 21. The penalties applicable separately, cumulatively or alternatively to legal entities, in accordance with the provisions of article 3, are: I — fine; II — restrictive of rights; III — provision of services to the community" (Brazil, 1998, p. 3).

such as: air, soil or water pollution; deforestation; climate change; and impacts on biodiversity.

Currently, the most serious injuries to the environment are predominantly caused by legal entities, which was found by the judge of the Court of Justice of Rio Grande do Sul, Eladio Lecey. It was even mentioned that the aforementioned injuries affect not only the individual interests of specific members or social groups, but also compromise essential legal goods, such as the preservation of life for current and future generations (Lecey, 1999, p. 171).

It is worth mentioning that, according to the jurist José Carlos Souza, when addressing the issue of damage to the environment, in cases where civil and administrative sanctions are not effective to deter the practice of infractions, the criminal liability of the business entity emerges as an essential counter-stimulus to prevent the perpetuation of criminal conducts that are harmful to society (Souza, 1988, p. 140).

Finally, Law No. 9,605/1998 is not the only one to typify conducts practiced by the business entity that generate liability in the criminal field, because Law No. 8,213/1991, which provides for Social Security Benefit Plans, imposed a criminal misdemeanor against the business entity in its article 19, paragraph 2, by mentioning that an accident at work that causes death or loss or reduction, permanent or temporary, of the ability to work, constitutes the aforementioned penalty, punishable by a fine.[7]

It is added that there would be compatibility of this provision, which establishes a criminal misdemeanor when the company fails to comply with

---

7 "Art. 19. An occupational accident is one that occurs due to the exercise of work in the service of a company or domestic employer or by the exercise of the work of the insured persons referred to in item VII of article 11 of this Law, causing bodily injury or functional disturbance that causes death or the loss or reduction, permanent or temporary, of the capacity to work" (Brazil, 1998, p. 9). Article 19, § 2: "It is a criminal misdemeanor, punishable by a fine, for the company to fail to comply with occupational safety and hygiene standards" (Brazil, 1998, p. 9).

the rules of safety and hygiene at work, with article 225, § 3, of the Federal Constitution. This is due to the fact that the regulation brought by Law No. 8,213/1991 would deal with the work environment.

In view of this, it is necessary to analyze the forms of criminal liability of the business entity, clarifying the theoretical and practical challenges, addressing the principle of personality of the sanction and finally the limitations in the application of punishment to the company.

LIMITATIONS AND COMPATIBILITY IN THE CRIMINAL LIABILITY OF LEGAL ENTITIES

Having overcome the issue of the theoretical foundation of the business entity and the criminal liability of the legal entity in the light of the Federal Constitution, it is necessary to analyze the forms of application of the sanction to companies, as well as the principle of the personality of the penalty, also known as personality, non-transcendence or non-transferability.

It is mentioned, from the beginning, with regard to the limitations of the sanction, that there are certain types that are subject to application to natural persons, however, they are incompatible with business entities. Illustratively, the prison sentence, which is applicable against individuals, has no correlated application to companies. Other punishments, however, are equally extended to both individuals and corporate entities, such as the application of fines. Finally, there are penalties that are exclusively compatible with business entities, such as the forced liquidation of the corporate entity.

In addition, regarding the principle of the personality of the penalty, it should be noted that it is intrinsically linked to the functions of the sanction in criminal law, ensuring that the application of punishments considers only the agent who committed the infraction, respecting its fundamental rights and promoting a more adequate and proportional justice. In this sense, it is emphasized that the aforementioned purposes are made for the agent who has not complied with the law, and are not pertinent to individuals who escape the infraction relationship. Therefore, the responsibility would have a personal responsibility, and cannot be extended to third parties who have not committed the crime.

In view of this, the analysis of the limitations in the application of the penalty is carried out, where the punishments compatible with the business entity will be analyzed.

Limitations in the Application of the Penalty

It is imperative, at this point, to explore the restrictions in the application of the penalty intended for business entities, bearing in mind the specificities intrinsic to corporate entities.

First, it should be mentioned that, because the privatization of liberty cannot be applied to companies, there was a need to restructure the system of criminal penalties. Thus, the entire criminal legal framework had to define the sanctions that would be levied on corporations, so that incompatibilities would not materialize.

In this sense, Law 9.605/1998, which deals with environmental crimes, brings a list of possible criminal sanctions to companies, being provided for in arts. 21 to 24 of the aforementioned law. In this sense, the punishments that restrict the rights of the business entity are: "partial or total suspension of activities; temporary interdiction of establishment, work or activity; and prohibition of hiring, obtaining subsidies, subsidies or donations from the Government". In addition, the provision of services to the community by the business entity will be those of "funding of environmental programs and projects, execution of works to recover degraded areas, maintenance of public spaces and contributions to public environmental or cultural entities". Finally, it can be noted that if the corporation is constituted or used, predominantly, for criminal purposes, it will have been decreed[8]

With regard to the limitations in the application of punishment to the business entity, it is observed that the penalties provided for include, essentially, fines, restrictions of rights and provision of services to the community, and may be used, in exceptional cases, the forced liquidation of the company.

Among the aforementioned penalties, the fine stands out, which, according to article 18 of the environmental crimes law, "will be calculated according to the criteria of the Penal Code; if it proves to be ineffective, even if applied at the maximum amount, it may be increased up to three times, in view of the value of the economic advantage obtained" (Brazil, 1998, p. 3).

It is mentioned that the Penal Code establishes strict criteria when dealing with the issue of setting the pecuniary punishment. Thus, article 49 of the CP deserves to be highlighted, which states that the aforementioned penalty

---

8 "Article 21. The penalties applicable separately, cumulatively or alternatively to business entities, in accordance with the provisions of article 3, are: I — fine; II — restrictive of rights; III — provision of services to the community" (Brazil, 1998, p. 3).

"Article 22. The penalties restricting the rights of the business entity are: I - partial or total suspension of activities; II - temporary interdiction of establishment, work or activity; III — prohibition of contracting with the Public Authority, as well as obtaining subsidies, subsidies or donations from it (...)" (Brazil, 1998, p. 3).

"Art. 23. The provision of services to the community by the business entity shall consist of: I — funding of environmental programs and projects; II — execution of works for the recovery of degraded areas; III — maintenance of public spaces; IV — contributions to public environmental or cultural entities" (Brazil, 1998, p. 3).

"Art. 24. The business entity constituted or used, preponderantly, with the purpose of allowing, facilitating or concealing the practice of a crime defined in this Law will have its forced liquidation decreed, its assets will be considered an instrument of the crime and as such forfeited in favor of the National Penitentiary Fund" (Brazil, 1998, p. 4).

will be calculated in fine days, being "at least 10 (ten) and at most 360 (three hundred and sixty)". In fact, the first paragraph of the same article mentions that the daily value "shall be fixed by the judge and may not be less than one-thirtieth of the highest monthly minimum wage in force at the time of the fact, nor more than five times that wage" (Brazil, 1940, p. 10).

It is also worth mentioning that, as stipulated by the law on environmental crimes, the CP was also concerned with special criteria for the penalty of a fine, by exposing in article 60, § 1, that, when defining this punishment, the economic situation of the defendant must be evaluated, so that it is possible to triple it, if the application of the sanction to the maximum is considered ineffective (Brazil, 1940).

In addition, it should be emphasized that the provision of services to the community by the business entity covers various activities related to environmental programs and projects, execution of works to recover degraded areas, maintenance of public spaces and contributions to public environmental or cultural entities. In addition, the law on crimes related to the environment establishes more severe measures, such as forced liquidation and the loss of assets in favor of the National Penitentiary Fund, in cases where the company is constituted or used predominantly with the purpose of allowing, facilitating or concealing the practice of crimes defined in the law in question (Brazil, 1998).

Additionally, according to Magistrate Vicente Maciel Júnior, the punishments exposed "must be applied as a way to prevent future unlawful acts, as well as to prevent damage to the environment and to diffuse stakeholders". In fact, according to the author, "it is certain that the penalty of suspension of activities or closure of the company should be applied as a last resort" (Júnior, 2022, p. 13).

In addition, the doctor of law, Cristina Ossipe Botelho, complements by saying that the sanctions applicable to corporate persons can be divided into two groups, pecuniary, as well as confiscation, which affect the assets of companies and those that affect activities, which would be in the first group.

In turn, in the second class, according to the author, there are alternative punishments, such as the prohibition of participation in public bids, removal of corporate leaders, disclosure of the conviction, suspension of operations and even the dissolution of the entity, together with the imposition of community service as a penalty (Botelho, 2004, p. 140).

In this way, this classification provides a more comprehensive understanding of the legal implications and options available in the context of criminal sanctions applied to business entities.

Adding the possibilities of punishments that can be imposed on companies, according to the doctrine of Judge Manoel Amorim, there would be other sanctions that can be imposed on corporate entities. According to the author, the main penalties, in addition to those mentioned in the legal text, are:

> a) Admonition or warning - consists of a true oral censure made by the Judge to the active subject considered guilty (...).
>
> c) Loss of property or confiscation - covers the illicit profit obtained by the offender, as well as the property acquired with the proceeds of the crime.
>
> d) Judicial injunction - as it is known in Portuguese law, it consists of putting an end to the duration of the unlawful act, obliging the agent to adopt the necessary measures to put an end to the anomalous situation. This type of penalty is appropriate for the so-called permanent crimes, whose consummation is prolonged in time (...).
>
> i) Disclosure of the sentence - it is made at the expense of the convicted legal entity, in the commercial establishment itself or in the place where its activities are carried out. Such a penalty produces more serious effects on the moral person than the fine imposed.
>
> j) Conditional suspension of sentence - in our law it can only replace the deprivation of liberty. It is also used in foreign law for

the non-execution of a punishment applied, provided that certain requirements are met.

1) Conditional suspension of the process - it is a measure that suspends the fact, even before the final decision itself (Amorim, 2000, p. 31).

Therefore, the aforementioned judge brought, in a non-exhaustive way, several other ways, which are not provided for in the current legislation on environmental crimes, to have the criminal punishment of a business entity. In this sense, measures such as the loss of assets or confiscation stand out, including the seizure of illicit profits and assets acquired with the proceeds from crime. Another important measure would be the disclosure of the sentence, carried out at the expense of the convicted company, occurs in the commercial establishment or place of activities, generating more serious effects than the fine, causing influence to the entire society on respect for the laws.

Thus, after discussing the limitations on the application of the penalty to business entities, it is necessary to analyze the principle of personality of punishment, which brings restrictive effects to the criminal conviction of the agent who committed the unlawful act. In this way, there will be scientific support for further analysis of the problems about the functions of the penalty in relation to the company.

Principle of the Personality of the Penalty

Also addressing the subject of limitations on the criminal liability of the business entity, which would be an obstacle to enter into the theme of the functions of punishment, it is worth making some comments about the principle of the personality of the penalty, also known as personality, intranscendence or non-transferability.

It is known that this principle considers the perpetrator of the crime in a particular way, promoting a proportional and appropriate sanction to the agent himself. Therefore, the core of the aforementioned legal basis is the identification of the person who committed a certain crime and only impute to that person the pertinent penalty, in light of the legislation in force and the actions carried out.

It turns out that imputing a punishment to a corporate entity does not necessarily imply the imposition of penalties on all its members. It is important to consider that, by treating the legal entity as an entity with its own life, it can be criminally liable independently of its members. Thus, even if it is necessary to hold the members individually responsible, each one will be liable to the extent of their participation or culpability.

In this vein, the Jurist Mourullo, asserts that "there capacity (...) of punishment presupposes the existence of a will in psychological-naturalistic terms, which, by definition, is the exclusive patrimony of individual persons" (Mourullo, 1978, p. 227-228).

Therefore, there is again the affirmation that criminal law, in the way it was constructed, based on the constitutionally established principles, aims to apply punishment to individuals. This is because, when punishing companies, one ends up punishing innocent individuals, which is not totally incompatible with the Personality of the Penalty.

It is worth mentioning that there is part of the doctrine, as clarified by the doctor of law Gianpaolo Poggio Smanio, who argues that the penalty, for the business entity, in the context addressed, is truly unconstitutional due to its transcendent nature, as it ends up affecting individuals who did not participate in the deliberation that culminated in the imposition of the sanction (Smanio, 2000).

Despite this, the criminal penalty, when applied to a corporation, does not necessarily reverberate on all its members. Society is, in fact, criminally responsible independently of its members.

The doctor in criminal law Cezar Roberto Bitencourt, clarifies, based on the lessons of Hassemer, a German judge, that there would be a need to create a legal branch, entitled as the right of intervention, positioning itself as an intermediate path between criminal law and administrative law, which dispenses with the application of severe sanctions of the legal system, notably the deprivation of liberty, however, it seeks effectiveness and offers less robust guarantees compared to traditional criminal law, in order to face the challenges of contemporary criminality, especially with regard to those committed by business entities (Bitencourt, 2003).

In this context, it is worth mentioning that, in relation to part of the doctrine, as stated by the jurist Cristina Botelho, the main arguments in favor of the company's criminal liability can be summarized in four: there is no capacity to be punished because there is no guilt; principle of personality; impossibility of repentance; and impossibility of deprivation of liberty (Botelho, 2004, p. 217).

However, even in the face of the personality of the punishments, the criminal liability of the business entity must be maintained. This is because, according to the principle, sanctions are applied considering the characteristics and individuality of the entity.

In this context, the Federal Constitution asserts, in article 5, items XLV and XLVI, that "no penalty shall pass from the person of the convicted" and that the "law shall regulate the individualization of the penalty", which is in line with the aforementioned principle (Federal Constitution, 1988, p. 4).

The CP complements the aforementioned by establishing that, in arts. 13 and 29, that "the result, on which the existence of the crime depends, is only imputable to the person who caused it" and that "whoever, in any way, contributes to the crime is subject to the penalties imposed on it, to the extent of their culpability" (Brazil, 1940, p. 3, 6).

In this context, the legal basis under analysis, enshrined in the Federal Constitution, presents itself as a support for the company's conception of criminal liability. By postulating that "no penalty shall pass from the person of the convicted" and providing for the aforementioned principle, the Constitution of the Republic emphasizes the need to link sanctions directly to the society that committed the unlawful act. This approach is compatible with the nature of corporations, given that they are endowed with their own legal capacity, with the imposition of personalized penalties (Federal Constitution, 1988, p. 4).

Even so, criminal law professor Fernando da Rocha clarifies that there is no one who can deny the reality that the family members of the convicted person experience adversities resulting from imprisonment or the impossibility of exercising a certain professional activity. In this context, the penalty has indirect repercussions on people who were not responsible for the practice of the infraction (Rocha, 1998).

The aforementioned professor complements by saying that, as far as the company is concerned, the penalty imposed on it will indirectly affect the partners or shareholders who, perhaps, have opposed the performance of the illegal activity. It should be noted that the FC, by enshrining, in item XLV of article 5, the provision that "no penalty shall pass from the person of the convicted" (Federal Constitution, 1988, p. 4), effectively establishes a restriction that binds the punishment to the violator of the law. Therefore, there is no contradiction to this precept in the context of society's responsibility, since the imposed restriction binds the punishment to the criminal, not requiring that he or she be the active subject of the crime (Rocha, 1998).

Even in view of Professor Fernando da Rocha's considerations, it is possible to conclude that the application of criminal liability to the company does not contradict the constitutional precept, since the penalty is linked to the person of the convicted, which in this case is society. Thus, the consequences of punishments led to a broader understanding of the relationship between the ability to be punished and its indirect impacts.

Finally, to illustrate what would be the lack of the principle of non-transferability of punishment in criminal law, we can cite the case of Tiradentes who, after being the target of the death penalty by hanging for the crime of high treason, for positioning himself against the Portuguese Crown, for the taxes collected and for the lack of independence of Minas Gerais in relation to the Empire, had his assets confiscated and his descendants, children and grandchildren were declared infamous. It should be mentioned that being "infamous" at the time was not just a title without any practical purpose, it represented moral torture for the people who received this appointment, including, the contempt was such that the house in which he lived was razed and salted, so that it would never be built on the ground again, so that no memory linked to that defendant would be preserved. However, this fact is not similar to the case of legal entities, since the individuals involved acted on their behalf, generating only a liability for the corporation (Tristão, 1999).

In view of this, it is also worth mentioning practical factors related to crimes committed by business entities. Thus, it is possible to mention that a joint analysis will be carried out of the speed with which the statute of limitations for environmental crimes occurs and the complexity related to major business damages. In addition, there will be a practical analysis of the Principle of Personality of the Penalty, with regard to corporate operations that involve corporate reorganization, as these generate the extinction of punishment in criminal law.

Theoretical and Practical Challenges

For all the foregoing in this subchapter of limitations and compatibility in the criminal liability of business entities, it is appropriate to confront other theoretical paradigms with the practical scenario.

Thus, for the doctrine, according to the PhD in law, Cristina Botelho, it is essential, in order for there to be the criminal liability of the business entity, the fulfillment of some criteria. First, it is imperative that the infringement was committed for the benefit of the company, and it is crucial that the unlawful action was performed by someone associated with the entity. In addition, it is essential that the infraction is related to the sphere of activity of the company, excluding those that are strictly within the competence of the individual, as in the case of bigamy. Finally, the infraction must involve the use of the power of the corporation, resulting in losses of greater intensity. These criteria outline the need for a direct connection between the infraction and the corporate dynamics, establishing clear limits for the criminal liability of the business entity and ensuring that the imputation of guilt falls proportionally and fairly in the organizational context (Botelho, 2004, p. 52).

In addition to the criteria outlined above, according to the professor of criminal law at the UFMG university, Fernando Galvão, there would be another requirement to be met in order to be able to hold the business entity criminally liable. This requirement concerns the type of company, because only the corporate entity of private law could see itself as a passive subject of an eventual action, since those of public law would not be covered by the types of punishment outlined by the ordinary legislator (Galvão, 2003).

However, the jurisprudence of the Federal Regional Court, of the 4th Region[9], presents an approach that contradicts the idea that only business entities governed by private law can be held criminally liable. The possibility of criminal liability of public entities is a reflection of the need to ensure the correctness of public administration and avoid impunity for acts that compromise administrative morality.

Thus, recent jurisprudence, according to the TRF-4, has advanced towards a broader interpretation, considering that criminal liability must be applied to all entities, regardless of their legal nature.

From the above, the complexity faced in the criminal prosecution of crimes committed by corporate entities becomes evident. This is due to the fact that, in order to have a correct complaint, it must be investigated extrajudicially

---

9 "TRF-4 - CRIMINAL APPEAL: ACR 50013165820184047121 RS 5001316-58.2018.4.04.712. 02/28/2019. Summary: ENVIRONMENTAL CRIME SUMMARY. (...). LEGAL ENTITY. PUBLIC LAW. POSSIBILITY. DOUBLE IMPUTATION. THEORY SUPERSEDED. (...) 3. The possibility of criminal liability of the business entity governed by Public Law is also supported by the case law of the Supreme Court. (...), the culpability of the bodies of the Public Power that violate the rules of Environmental Criminal Law can be especially considered". Rapporteur: Giovani Bigolin (TRF-4. (2019). Criminal Appeal: ACR 50013165820184047121. RS 5001316-58.2018.4.04.712. 02/28/2019).

whether the infraction was committed for the benefit of the company, by someone associated with it.

In fact, because there is the use of the company's power, resulting in losses of greater intensity, it makes it very difficult to fully investigate the environmental crimes perpetrated. The extent of the environmental damage, notably due to the affected territorial amplitude and the diversity of impacted ecosystems, greatly amplifies the difficulty inherent to the investigation. The plurality of affected individuals, whether they are local communities, fauna or flora, adds a level of complexity, since the identification and quantification of the damage requires detailed and specialized analyses. In addition, the future consequences resulting from environmental damage may have long-term implications, requiring a prospective approach in the assessment of impacts. The identification and individualization of the people involved in the practice of environmental illegality, whether managers, employees or third-party collaborators, is another considerable challenge, especially when there are complex corporate structures.

In view of these circumstances, the complexity inherent in the investigation of environmental crimes perpetrated by a business entity is clearly noted, as it is manifested by an interconnection of factors that require technical expertise and multidisciplinary efforts for the effective elucidation of the facts and adequate accountability.

In this sense, in view of the complexity inherent in the investigation of environmental crimes perpetrated by legal entities, a concern arises regarding the statute of limitations for these crimes. The delay in completing the investigations can hinder not only the initial stage of the work, but can impact the intercurrent statute of limitations, that is, when there is already a certain criminal case in progress, it can also be seen as a risk to be faced.

As for a practical example in the Brazilian context, we can cite the Samarco case, which occurred on November 5, 2015, with the rupture of the dam in the rural area of Mariana, Minas Gerais (MG). This event caused the release of mining tailings, in order to devastate places such as Paracatu de Baixo and

Camargos, the cities of Barra Longa, Rio Doce and Santa Cruz do Escalvado and communities in the East of Minas, such as Governador Valadares. The tailings also contaminated Espírito Santo, carried by the Rio Doce River, affecting Regência, Linhares, Baixo Gandu and Colatina. In summary, the tailings destroyed the subdistrict of Santa Rita Durão, Bento Rodrigues, and more than 40 cities in Minas Gerais and Espírito Santo (D'Agostino, 2015).

In this case, 362 families were left homeless and 19 people died. According to Ibama, it was estimated that 50 million cubic meters were affected by this waste. According to Duarte Júnior, mayor of Mariana, the damage is about 100 million Reals, accounting for environmental damage, infrastructure, bridges and destroyed schools. The mayor also claimed that 80% of the amount collected by the city comes from mining at the Germano Unit, circulating nine million Reals monthly in Tax on the Circulation of Goods and Services (ICMS; D'Agostino, 2015).

With regard to the aforementioned Samarco case, two environmental crimes, provided for in Law 9.605/98, have already expired due to the aforementioned procedural slowness. Specifically, the crimes outlined in articles 49 and 50 of the aforementioned law, which cover the destruction, damage, injury or mistreatment of ornamental plants and the devastation of native or planted forests, respectively, are now time-barred. The seriousness of these acts, linked to the context of the aforementioned dam failure, is accentuated by the imminence that crimes against flora may also prescribe in the year 2024, increasing concerns about the effectiveness of the criminal response in the face of the environmental impacts resulting from the aforementioned disaster.

It is worth mentioning that articles 49 and 50, of Law 9.605/98, each of them provides for detention from three months to one year. From this scenario, it is known that it is up to the PC to regulate the limitation periods of the entire Brazilian legal system, which it does in article 109, which says "the statute of limitations, before the final sentence becomes final, except as provided for in § 1 of article 110 of this Code, is regulated by the maximum of the deprivation of liberty committed to the crime, verifying: V - in four years, if the maximum sentence is equal to one year or, if it is higher, does not exceed two" (Brazil, 1940, p. 22).

In addition, it is relevant to deal with the case of Brumadinho, MG, which occurred on January 25, 2019, under the responsibility of the mining company Vale. On the occasion in question, the dam of the Córrego do Feijão Mine was ruptured and, consequently, 272 people died, in addition to toxic ore residues scattered throughout the Paraopeba River basin. According to the president of the aforementioned company, there were 12 million cubic meters of tailings, with an estimated reach of 200 km in area, reaching the São Francisco River. The waste went down the Serra dos Dois Irmãos, in order to reach the Paraopeba River, which supplies a third of the metropolitan region of Belo Horizonte, and flowed into the São Francisco River (Mansur, 2023).

It is known, then, that the Brumadinho case faced significant challenges regarding the time lapse for the statute of limitations, notably when, just two days before the statute of limitations for environmental crimes. This is because, they were subject to a four-year term, as well as the collapse of the dam in Mariana, the Federal Public Prosecutor's Office formalized a complaint before the Federal Court (Zuba, 2023).

Another topic that deserves to be highlighted concerns corporate transactions involving the reorganization of companies and their link with the principle of personality. The analysis of these transactions in the light of this legal basis is essential, since such reorganizations can directly influence the criminal liability of corporate entities. Issues pertaining to the continuity of the business entity, the extent of the effects of the punishment on the reorganized entity and the possibility of mitigating or transferring the capacity to be punished are crucial aspects.

Corporate operations related to business reorganization comprise mergers, incorporations, spin-offs and transformations. In the merger, two or more companies unite to create a new entity, resulting in the extinction of the preexisting business entities. In the merger, one entity absorbs another, resulting in the dissolution of the merged company and the transfer of its assets to the developer. The spin-off, in turn, consists of the fragmentation of a pre-existing entity into multiple independent entities, each absorbing a fraction of the original assets. Transformation, the last modality, refers to the change in the legal structure of an entity without, however, impacting the legal personality.

In this context, when the company responsible for the environmental crime is extinguished in the physical sphere, either because it has gone through a process of merger, incorporation or total spin-off, the principle of personality gives rise to the extinction of the previous liability associated with the environmental crime perpetrated. This is because, since sanctions are strictly personal, one cannot go beyond the society that committed them.

This is the current understanding of the Third Section of the Supreme Court of Justice (STJ), where the criminal liability of a company is in no way transferred with incorporation. The Third Section, by majority vote, decided that the capacity of the acquired company to be criminally punished cannot be transferred to the acquiring company. The panel established the understanding that the aforementioned constitutional principle can be applied to business entities, thus generating the termination of the punishability.

The understanding of the Third Section of the Supreme Court of Justice (STJ) reflects an important decision on the criminal liability of companies in the context of mergers. The majority decision established that criminal culpability is not automatically transferred to the acquiring company. This position is based on constitutional principles and aims to ensure clarity and proper application of the rules of criminal liability in the business sphere. Therefore, the acquiring company cannot be held criminally liable for the unlawful acts committed by the acquired company, unless there are other circumstances that justify such liability.

It turns out that the decision may directly affect society's expectations regarding the criminal liability of collective entities. When a company commits criminal conduct, it is natural for society to expect that company to be held accountable for its acts, either through fines, administrative sanctions or, in more serious cases, criminal liability. However, if the application of criminal liability is hampered or limited by judicial interpretations that restrict the automatic transfer of responsibilities in incorporation proceedings, this can lead to frustration and distrust in the judicial system.

Therefore, it is crucial that judicial decisions like this are critically analyzed, considering not only the legal principles involved, but also the social impacts and the maintenance of legal certainty. The consequences of these precedents can significantly shape the legal and business environment, influencing how businesses operate and how fairness is perceived by society as a whole.

It is worth mentioning that, according to a report carried out by journalists Heliana Gonçalves and Roberta Batista, also on the Pinheiro Case, it became known after an earthquake in some neighborhoods of Maceió, Municipality of Alagoas, in March 2018. Braskem is a company that extracts rock salt, an ore used in the manufacture of caustic soda and PVC, at a depth of 390 meters below the surface. However, it is known that a possible rupture of the mine of the aforementioned society could impact the Mundaú lagoon, in which it is used as the main source of income for fishermen and sururu harvesters. In addition, it is possible to see earth movement at the site, since there was no preparation for extraction. Therefore, a possible collapse has been predicted, which would generate a crater at the site. Until December 2023, the news was that the earth had sunk 2.35 meters (Gonçalves, 2023).

Another relevant fact, brought by the aforementioned report is that, "although there is concern about a greater salinization of the lagoon, pollution in the region is still the most serious problem". In addition, it was reported about the collection of water samples made bimonthly that "pointed out that the lagoon is polluted by sewage, pesticides and other contaminating substances". Finally, it is mentionable that, according to the aforementioned journalists, "the interdiction at sea has also affected those who work with tourist tours in the lagoon", making catamaran owners feel that the tours are bringing together fewer and fewer people, not even reaching 50% of capacity (Gonçalves, 2023, p. 3-7).

It turns out that news has been spreading through the national media about the future sale of Braskem, which may exempt new owners from paying for the mining company's crimes. It is worth mentioning that the criminal liability of individuals would remain inert, however, the aforementioned capacity of companies to be punished may be extinguished depending on how this sale or incorporation takes place. This is due to the fact that, as mentioned earlier, there is a precedent in the Third Section of the STJ in this regard, although there is, as mentioned above, some divergence in the doctrine and in the court itself (Martins, 2023, p. 3).

Thus, it is crucial to consider legal alternatives that ensure the continuity of the company's criminal liability, even under new management. One way out would be the stipulation of specific contractual clauses during the sale or merger process, which provide for the assumption of pre-existing criminal responsibilities by the new entity or its owners. An alternative would be the adoption of legislative measures that ensure the transfer of criminal obligations to the successor company, regardless of the contractual conditions agreed. In addition, a continuity of legal liability could be imposed, recognizing that the business entity retains its identity and legal obligations even under new ownership.

It is worth remembering that the decision may directly affect society's expectations regarding the criminal liability of companies. If judicial interpretations restrict the transfer of responsibilities in incorporation processes, this can undermine trust in the judicial system. Therefore, it is important to consider not only the legal principles, but also the social impacts and legal certainty.

In summary, the complexities inherent to the criminal liability of business entities, outlined by the doctrinal criteria and specific requirements, reveal themselves as significant obstacles in the effective prosecution of crimes committed by corporate entities. In fact, there is a real concern with the statute of limitations, evidenced in the Samarco and Brumadinho cases, highlighting the urgency of measures to avoid impunity in the face of catastrophic environmental events. In fact, the practical concern of corporate transactions in relation to the principle of personality was highlighted, which raises concerns regarding the company's ability to be punished, in this scenario, the context of Braskem was cited.

After the explanation of the theoretical and practical challenges regarding the limitations and compatibility in the criminal liability of the business entity, the need to address the functions of punishment and the relationship with the company emerges. In this context, it is vital to analyze not only the theories on which these purposes are based, but also the evolution of these guidelines and possible practical implications for the ability to be punished.

FUNCTIONS OF THE PENALTY AND THE RELATIONSHIP WITH THE BUSINESS ENTITY

Once the theoretical foundation and the criminal liability of the business entity have been overcome, it is necessary to analyze the functions of the penalty and the direct relationship with the business entity. Thus, it is also important to highlight some points that deserve future legislative improvement, as well as certain practical analyses.

The functions of punishment are presented as legitimizing pillars of criminal intervention in society and justify why there is the application of sanctions to those who commit infractions. Therefore, punitive law is not understood by the law and the constitution as an end in itself, an application without logical or rational basis, because it was built aiming mainly at two purposes, retribution and prevention, which will be explored in this chapter.

In this sense, to achieve the aforementioned purpose, there are two guidelines that stand out and underlie the functions of punishment, namely, the absolute and relative theory. At the outset, it is important to inform that they do not deal with only one absolute and one relative strand, as there are several doctrinal currents explaining each of them, with certain divergences, which are thus often called absolute and relative. As it is not the purpose of this work to analyze each absolute and each relative aspect, the most accepted points of each view will be considered, therefore, extremist positions will not be treated.

According to the Brazilian jurist Aníbal Bruno, the theories of sanction "serve to justify the punitive measure, to elucidate its essence and its objectives, they serve the same purposes in relation to criminal law" (Bruno, 2009, p.12).

Today, it is possible to affirm that the configuration of criminal law is closely linked to the results it is expected to achieve, both in relation to the individual who is the target of the State's action and to the society in which it operates. In addition, there is practically a consensus within the scope of the science of the aforementioned legal branch that punishment is justified by indispensability.

It is worth mentioning at the outset that the functions of punishment are not linked in a single way to a branch of law, as Criminal Law, however, it is in harmony with each type of sanction provided for in the legislative sphere. Therefore, the aforementioned purposes do not only draw connections with Criminal Law, but are also linked to the deprivation of freedom, restrictions of rights, fines and services to the community, each with its own theory that justifies it, both the absolute and the relative aspects.

Finally, the theme of absolute theory and debates related to companies deserves analysis now, aiming to understand the aforementioned guideline and explore in depth its relations with the corporate entity. Therefore, the problems and difficulties related to the theme will be explored.

ABSOLUTE THEORY AND DEBATES RELATED TO COMPANIES

The absolute theory, also called retributivist, is the first pillar that justifies the function of punishment in Brazilian criminal law. Thus, it is known that this strand, in a great way, was influenced by the lessons of the German philosopher Immanuel Kant, and, from this thought, it was perfected for the current conception.

According to the German philosopher, Immanuel Kant, a relevant specificity of punishment was highlighted, its species and measure. These two details were reflected by the aforementioned philosopher, leading him to conclude that the ius talionis, that is, the Law of Talion, was presented as the best option, as long as the conception of morality of the society in question agrees with the retributive punishment. Thus, for the philosopher, the unjust action directed at another person, in fact, would affect the agent who committed the crime, according to its species and measure.

However, for Kant, although the quantity and quality of punishment is regulated according to the Law of Talion, the final judgment of each case could not be made by a common individual of society, but always by a specific court designated for that situation. Finally, the great value given to the retributionist theory established by the aforementioned philosopher arises in the issue of establishing a limitation to the penal imposition, that is, there are maximum limits that each agent who has broken the law can be punished, these limits are directly linked to the harm caused, and the criminal agent cannot be punished more severely than the evil committed. This consideration arose from the principle of individual freedom and the dignity of the human person.

It is worth mentioning that, according to Judge Antonio Camargo, in the absolute theory, punishment is consecrated as a retribution for the evil done by the agent, punitur quia peccatum est, in a literal translation, the agent will be punished because he has sinned. In this way, the penalty will be assigned according to the culpability of each offender. It is appropriate to add that the sanction only takes place after the practice of the criminal act, symbolizing a punishment for the delinquent (Camargo, 2002, p. 205).

Thus, it can be considered that Kantian philosophy presupposes that the offender is liable to be punished, since the subject must suffer in a similar way to the harm caused. However, when dealing with a business entity, according to the Kantian theory, because it is an abstract entity, not endowed with the biopsychological element, there would be no way to discuss the applicability of the penalty in a similar way to the harm caused, nor about the moral punishment.

The criminologist Juarez Cirino dos Santos corroborates the aforementioned statement by claiming that the application of retributivism is ineffective in the case of a legal entity, since repentance or affection presupposes the existence of a conscious being (Santos, 2010, p. 281).

However, after the elaboration of the penal dogmatics, retribution began to be treated as the legal response to the crime, in order to be detached from a moral reaction to the crime. In this way, the corporate entity is seen as a being that has a will and, thus, can be blamed independently of the physical entities associated with it.

In this sense, the theory of retribution does not attribute to punishment any purpose other than being an end in itself, exuding only the compensatory character, of receiving for oneself what one has practiced against third parties, which represents the very consequence of the crime. In this context, the absolute aspect is characterized by independence and detachment from the purpose of punishment from any social effect. Therefore, the characteristic of the absolute is that the only justification for the existence of the sanction would be the fact that it confers on the one who practiced a typical conduct the retribution of his own evil.

It should be said that it was sought to maintain only the essence of the absolute theory developed by Kant, from this, many punishments were limited, regulated or transformed. In this sense, the Federal Constitution establishes in its article 5, item XLVII, that "there shall be no penalties: a) death (...); b) of a perpetual nature; c) forced labor; d) banishment; e) cruel" (Federal Constitution, 1988, p. 4).

Thus, forms that were accepted that violated physical or moral integrity, punished in perpetuity, forced him to perform forced labor, banished or were even cruel to the agent who committed a fact defined as a crime, were no longer accepted as a lawful form of punishment. In this sense, the Penal Code asserts, in its article 32, that the sanctions that are possible for individuals are: "I — deprivation of liberty; II — restrictive of rights; III — of a fine" (Brazil, 1940, p. 6).

In view of this scenario outlined by the Federal Constitution, in which the sanctions provided for, with the exception of deprivation of liberty, are subject to imposition on business entities, their criminal liability was constitutionally authorized. In this sense, the possible punishments for corporate entities are provided for in Law 9,605/1998, in article 21, which reads as follows: "I — fine; II — restrictive of rights; III — provision of services to the community" (Brazil, 1998, p. 3).

It is imperative to highlight that not only would there be functions of the penalty in criminal liability as a way to justify the application of any punishment, however, each of those legislatively provided for must exude the purpose it seeks. Therefore, these purposes not only justify Criminal Law as a whole, demonstrating that it would meet the Absolute or Relative Theory, which will be assessed, but rather, they must be linked to each possible sanctioning species.

In this sense, the deprivation of freedom, the fine, the restriction of rights and the provision of services to the community must, each species, be related to at least one theory of the functions of punishment.

The deprivation of freedom has a dual role in terms of the function of its application, at first it has the purpose of retribution, but it also has the purpose of preventing new crimes. It so happens that, when analyzing the sanctions that are compatible with the business entity, the referred punishment is not appropriate, due to physical incompatibility.

Regarding the pecuniary punishment, this, according to the doctrine, supported by criminal lawyer Marina Coelho Araújo, has a retributive bias, aiming to penalize the agent in proportion to the seriousness of the offense committed. It should also be noted that, according to the aforementioned lawyer, although the fine does not have the greatest importance with regard to the conviction of individuals, since this role is attributed to the deprivation of liberty. It happens that, when it comes to companies, financial penalties play a role of excellence, making the entire sanctioning system of collective entities revolve around the punishment of the former (Coelho Araújo, 2017, p. 183).

With regard to the other types of sanctions brought by Law 9.605/1998, namely, the penalties restricting rights and those of community service, these, in fact, reveal an attribute of a more preventive nature. Thus, the aforementioned criminal punishments would not be directly linked to the Absolute Theory of the Function of Punishment, not serving the purpose of repaying the perpetrator of the offense for the evil committed by him (Coelho Araújo, 2017, p. 183).

Thus, in the light of the current absolute theory, perfected from the teachings of the philosopher Kant, it would actually be possible to hold the company criminally liable, at least at a theoretical level, bearing in mind that the fine would be assigned the role of compensation. It should be mentioned that, with regard to the practical aspect, it lacks analysis, based on several pragmatic expressions of law in relation to the theme studied here, as well as comparisons between the application of the remuneration chain for individuals and for companies.

In this scenario, with regard to the practical aspect of the Absolute Theory, it is worth noting that article 59 of the Penal Code indicates that the sanction must be necessary and sufficient for the disapproval of the crime, establishing the applicable amount, within the limits provided. It is known, therefore, that the sanction should aim at punishing the agent, generating in him a feeling that the act practiced is in fact reprehensible and deserves to be punished, because there was damage from the practice of the crime (Brazil, 1940).

It should be noted that the penalty, in the light of the absolute theory, aims to punish the agent for the offense committed, instilling in the transgressor a feeling that, in fact, there was a reprehensibility that will be felt by him, either with the restriction of freedom or with the restriction of rights, or by the imposition of patrimonial loss or the provision of services to the community. In this sense, the application of the penalty not only reflects the imposition of a sanction resulting from the ethical disapproval of the conduct, but the person of the agent who is being punished must be considered, so that the quantity aligned with the emergence of the feeling of reproach is improved, seeking to rebalance the equation of justice in the face of the damage caused to society, thus reinforcing the importance of maintaining the legal order.

It should be said that the Penal Code carries in its core principles aligned with the absolute theory, by establishing punishments proportional to the seriousness of the crime. Even for exceptional situations, it brings special criteria with the main objective of correcting the breach of the aforementioned proportionality, such as article 60, § 1, which, when defining the fine, the economic situation of the defendant must be ascertained, in order to know if the punishment, even applied to the maximum, would prove to be ineffective, in this case, it would be possible to triple it (Brazil, 1940).

Still on the subject of penalties proportional to the seriousness of the crime, it is worth mentioning article 6 of Law No. 9,605 of 1998, item III, which states that the competent authority must observe the economic situation of the offender in the case of a fine.[10]

In this sense, it is possible to extract from the essence of the aforementioned articles a marked concern of the criminal legislation when the core of the trial concerns a punishment linked to the economic part of the offender. Therefore, when a certain legal issue deals with the criminal liability of the offender with his own assets, it should be emphasized that the criminal legislation is too concerned with analyzing the economic situation of the defendant, seeking to know whether the penalty would prove to be ineffective in the specific case.

It should be added that, when faced with the quantification of the amount that will be owed by a company for having committed a criminal act, in the same way that an individual will have the economic situation ascertained, so must the business entity. Therefore, the crux of the matter lies in analyzing proportionality when the issue of a fine is under trial in criminal proceedings.

10 "Art. 6 For the imposition and gradation of the penalty, the competent authority shall observe:" (Brazil, 1998, p. 1). Article 6, III: "the economic situation of the offender, in the case of a fine" (Brazil, 1998, p. 1).

In this context, mention can be made of the principle of individualization of the penalty, which is not to be confused with that of the personality of the sanction. That is a fundamental concept, showing that there is a need to personalize punishment according to the specific circumstances of each agent. From the aforementioned legal basis, the uniqueness of each concrete case must be recognized, considering several factors that are related to criminal activity, including factors related to the accused itself. This is due to the fact that there is a search for the security that the penalty has proportionality and justice, understood as equality, reasonableness and impartiality.

Regarding the Samarco Case, which had already been analyzed by the present work, which consisted, in summary, in the rupture of a dam in the rural area of Mariana, MG, causing the release of 50 million cubic meters of mining tailings, which devastated more than 40 cities. In fact, according to Duarte Júnior, mayor of Mariana, the loss would be around 100 million Reals (D'Agostino, 2015).

In addition, in the civil sphere, as pointed out by journalist Wendal Carmoa, the Federal Court of Minas Gerais sentenced the mining companies Vale, BHP and Samarco to pay the amount of 47.6 billion Reals in compensation for collective moral damages resulting from the collapse of the Fundão dam, in Mariana. In this way, the damage caused by the dam collapse would be compatible with the total amount of 47.6 billion Reals. The journalist also pointed out that the amount will still be corrected with interest from the date of the tragedy, which occurred on November 5, 2015, and may reach the amount of 73 billion, as civil liability (Carmoa, 2024).

In this sense, with regard to the purpose of this indemnity, the Civil Code clarifies, in arts. 186 and 927, header, that anyone who violates rights and causes damage to others, even if it is only of a moral nature, commits an unlawful act. In addition, it mentions that, when committing an unlawful act, causing damage to third parties, it is obliged to repair it.[11]

Therefore, when violating rights and causing damage to a third party, even if it is moral, he commits an unlawful act, and for committing an unlawful act, it must make reparation. In this sense, it is worth mentioning article 944 of the same Code, which states that compensation is measured by the extent of the damage, and if there is an excessive disproportion between the seriousness of the fault and the damage, it may equitably reduce the compensation (Brazil, 2002).

Therefore, the purpose of civil indemnity, that is, the function of civil indemnity, is to repair the damage caused. In this way, there is truly a search for the state in which the business was moments before the damage occurred, which is represented by the Latin expression status quo. With regard to moral damage, there would be the incidence of the pretium doloris, which is the price of pain, thus, there would be the responsibility to pay a certain amount that is proportional to the damage that was suffered by the third parties.

Thus, the function of civil indemnity, in simple terms, would be the demand for compensation for the damages suffered, not having in its essence the intention of punishment. As a result, there will only be an assessment of the amount of compensation seeking to compensate for the losses that a certain third party suffered. It should be added that the indemnity will be calculated from the loss actually incurred, which is the emerging damage, as well as what the injured party failed to earn or profit from the harmful event, which is treated by the aforementioned Code as loss of profit.

---

11 "Article 186. Anyone who, by voluntary action or omission, negligence or imprudence, violates rights and causes damage to others, even if exclusively moral, commits an unlawful act" (Brazil, 2002, p. 16). "Article 927. Anyone who, by an unlawful act (articles 186 and 187), causes damage to another, is obliged to repair it" (Brazil, 2002, p. 67).

Therefore, civil liability aims at pecuniary compensation in accordance with the extent of the damage caused, and its primary purpose, through indemnity, is not to raise the retribution of the damage to the offending agent, even generating the feeling of reproach, as a reaction to the initially reprehensible conduct, which is what happens in criminal law. This time, the difference between the function of punishment for criminal law and the purpose of compensation for civil law becomes evident.

Regarding the importance of reparation for victims in the context of restorative justice, especially in cases of economic crimes, the relevance of measures such as precautionary blocking and forfeiture of assets, as provided for in articles 4 and 7 of Law 9,613/98, which must be carried out without delay and without prior knowledge of the investigated, is highlighted. In fact, the victim's compensation not only fulfills the role of repairing the damage suffered, but also strengthens the principle of restorative justice, promoting the reparation of the social and economic impacts of the crime (Law 9.613, 1998, p. 3, 5).

Another issue that must be assessed concerns the administrative fine that deals with the manifestation of the State's power to investigate, when the subject deals with environmental administration. The legal provision for administrative liability is found in article 70 of Law 9.605/98, which states that "any action or omission that violates the legal rules of use, enjoyment, promotion, protection and recovery of the environment is considered an environmental administrative infraction" (Brazil, 1998, p. 11-12).

Furthermore, environmental administrative liability aims to ensure compliance with and observance of environmental standards and regulations by individuals or business entities that may cause negative impacts on the environment. In this way, it seeks to ensure the protection, conservation and preservation of natural resources, as well as the prevention and repair of environmental damage.

It should be noted that, with regard to the function of applying a certain penalty in the administrative sphere, it is equivalent to the criminal sphere, being justified by seeking to prevent certain damage from occurring or to repair certain environmental damage that has already occurred. Thus, both administrative and criminal liability have the same justification for the application of the sanction, however, they are different with regard to what they aim to protect, on the one hand, punitive legislation seeks to protect the most relevant legal assets of society and on the other hand, administrative law seeks to protect the environment through various regulations that need to be followed.

It so happens that the ordinary legislator, when defining monetary limits for the application of the environmental administrative fine, asserted that it could only be established between a minimum of 50 Reals and a maximum of 50 million Reals for each administrative infraction committed. It is worth mentioning that the pecuniary punishment may be simple, where it will have only one application, or it may be daily, a situation in which it will be applied whenever the infraction extends over time, with the maximum amount pre-established by the legislator as a total limit (Brazil, 1998).

In this sense, in the Samarco Case, considering only the disaster that occurred, Ibama, which is the institute responsible for the fines applied to the aforementioned situation, only had the possibility of notifying the mining company five times, for having committed five different damage events to the environment. Regarding these five notifications, journalist Rosanne D'Agostino clarified that they were due to "water pollution resulting in a risk to human health, making urban areas unsuitable for occupation, causing interruption of the public water supply, throwing waste in disagreement with legal requirements and causing the death of animals and the loss of biodiversity along the Rio Doce River" (D'Agostino, 2015, p. 13).

In this context of application of only five notifications, each of them was assigned the maximum degree of the fine, resulting in the amount of 250 million Reals. In addition, after the fact, another 20 infraction notices were filed to correct minor situations, more that resulted from the dam failure, which, when added to the previous five, resulted in pecuniary punishments in the amount of 350.7 million Reals to the mining company. This was the total amount applied by Ibama in the Samarco Case, however, it is worth mentioning that it is a punitive debt, which aims to repay all the disasters that occurred as a result of the dam failure to the mining company, thus seeking to bring the feeling of disapproval, in response to the previous disapproval practiced.

It is worth noting that, when comparing the environmental administrative fine, which aims to punish the agent in the proportion in which he caused the damage, with the civil indemnity applied to the case, the former is far behind, since, in fact, 350.7 million Reals represent approximately 0.738% of 47.6 billion Reals, which would correspond to the estimated amount of damage that was caused. Therefore, the administrative fine, used to repress the mining company Samarco for the disaster it caused, did not reach the level of 1% of the damage caused.

It is also necessary to analyze the criminal sphere, in relation to the Samarco Case, which may also impose fines to be paid by the mining company. It should be noted that the sanction aims to repay the offending agent for the harm caused by him.

In this scenario, it is worth briefly highlighting the maximum limits in the application of the penalty, in relation to the fine in the criminal sphere. According to the law on environmental crimes, the criterion brought by the Penal Code will be applied, however, if it is ineffective, it can be increased up to three times. In this sense, the CP points out that the pecuniary punishment will be calculated in fine days, with a maximum of 360. Regarding the amount, it cannot exceed the minimum wage in force at the time of the fact, by five times. In addition, the aforementioned law established that it would be possible to triple the amount of that penalty if it is considered ineffective (Brazil, 1940).

In the criminal proceeding proposed as a result of the Mariana Case, in addition to the individuals denounced, as evidenced by journalist Pablo Nascimento, the Brazilian mining company Samarco is responsible for 10 environmental crimes (articles 29, 33, 38, 38-A, 40, 54, 62, 68, 69 and 69-A of Law 9.605/1998). It should also be noted that the shareholders of the aforementioned company, the Brazilian multinational mining company

Vale S.A., will also be liable for the same 10 environmental crimes, and the mining company BHP Billiton Brazil, was denounced for seven environmental crimes (articles 29, 33, 38, 38-A, 40, 54 and 62 of Law 9,605/1998). Finally, the engineering company VogBR Recursos Hidros was denounced for only one environmental crime (art. 69-A, § 2, of Law 9.605/1998; Nascimento, 2023).

In this context, it is possible to determine the quantum that would be due to the maximum by all the companies denounced, in view of the limitations brought by the criminal legislation. When specifically examining the imputations directed to the mining company Samarco, which had 10 crimes imputed against it, the maximum possible sanction would be the result of the sum of five minimum wages, at the time of the facts, therefore five times 788 Reals, multiplied by 360, for each day-fine, tripled, for being ineffective according to the punitive code, times three, for being ineffective according to the Environmental Crimes Law and tenfold, for having been the defendant denounced for 10 crimes, resulting in an amount of R$127,656,000.00.

At this point, it should be noted that, according to the absolute theory of the function of punishment, the sanction is consecrated as a compensation for the harm done by the agent, aiming to punish him for having practiced damage before society. It is worth mentioning that the retribution guideline exudes the compensatory character, of receiving for oneself what one has practiced against third parties, which represents the very consequence of the crime. In fact, according to article 59 of the Penal Code, the penalty must be necessary and sufficient for the disapproval of the crime. Consequently, punishment aims to instill in the transgressor a feeling that, in fact, there was a reproach that will be felt by it.

Another aspect that is worth mentioning deals with the concern of the Penal Code with regard to the analysis of the person of the agent who is being punished, so that the amount of punishment is improved, seeking to rebalance the equation of justice in the face of the damage caused to society. Even when it comes to a punishment linked to the patrimonial part, it is necessary to analyze, according to the punitive code, the economic situation of the defendant, seeking to know if the penalty would prove to be ineffective in the specific case, so that there is proportionality when the issue of fine is under trial.

Thus, the criminal law, which has as justification for the application of the sanction the absolute theory, would condemn at most the Samarco company, for the catastrophe that occurred from the collapse of the dam, for the 10 crimes committed, in R$ 127,656,000.00. At this moment, when dealing with the R$127,656,000.00, which symbolizes the maximum degree that said company would respond to, it represents approximately 0.2684% of the estimated damage that was caused, which would be the amount of 47.6 billion Reals.

In this sense, the punishment that aims to compensate for the damage caused to the offender itself, would apply a fine of a maximum of 0.2684% of the value of the damage caused. This fact does not generate any reproach to the perpetrator of the crime, and is not able to express in any way the practical purpose that is sought with the absolute theory. It can be observed that there is only the theoretical provision that there would be a compensatory character by the criminal legislation, however, from a practical point of view, it could not be truthfully stated that there was a retribution for the harm caused to the criminal as a business entity.

In this sense, it is possible to affirm that there was a criminal conduct that harmed several legal assets essential to society, but, due to all the limitations regarding the punishment of the offender as a business entity, it would not, in a proportional manner, be condemned, only to repair what, as civil compensation, the damages caused. Therefore, there would be no reprimand for the damage caused, serving as retribution for environmental catastrophes, even if they are assets of extreme importance for the law.

In addition, it can be pointed out that there would be another way to analyze the case, not based on the damage that had been caused, but by how much, according to the economic condition of the defendant company, would be enough to generate in it the feeling of reproach. In this sense, it is worth mentioning that, according to the printed magazine Brazil Mineral, in 2022,

Samarco's adjusted managerial Ebitda, which refers to earnings before taxes, interest and depreciation, reached 4.82 billion Reals (Brazil Mineral, 2023).

Thus, considering that the Samarco company receives 4.82 billion Reals in profit per year, and would have to pay R$127,656,000.00 to pay the punitive fine imposed by the criminal sphere, it would be the same as removing approximately 2.65% from the company's annual profit. In practical terms, the pecuniary punishment stipulated in criminal law would be compatible with what the company earns every 10 days. It is also worth mentioning the administrative punishment, as it has a corrective purpose similar to criminal law, which was calculated at 350.7 million Reals, which would require around 26 days for total liquidation, according to the annual profit of the mining company.

Therefore, when analyzing the amount that will be determined as a criminal sanction in comparison with the damage caused or even with the annual profit of the Samarco company, it is possible to show that the criminal punishment is insufficient to meet the purposes it seeks, which is to impose on the agent a penalty compatible with the harm done, generating a retribution for the damage caused.

The Samarco Case is not considered an isolated fact in the national scenario, the same occurred with the one in Brumadinho, under the responsibility of the mining company Vale. It should be noted that in this specific situation, the dam of the Córrego do Feijão Mine was ruptured and, consequently, 12 million cubic meters of toxic ore tailings were scattered.

In the Brumadinho Case, as reported by reporter Heloísa Mendonça, Vale signed an agreement to pay 37.68 billion Reals as reparation for the tragedy that occurred. In this sense, it is worth mentioning that this debt does not include any punishment for the acts performed, it consists only of amounts referring to compensation for everything that happened, seeking the status quo (Mendonça, 2021).

In this context, there was the application of the environmental administrative fine, Ibama, which is the institute responsible for applying administrative penalties in the Brumadinho Case, applied a pecuniary punishment to Vale in the amount of 250 million Reals. In this scenario, it should be noted that the administrative sanction plays a fundamental role in punishing the business entity that committed administrative infractions, thus aiming to correct the company that broke the law, so that it receives a punishment compatible with the damage caused.

Thus, it is necessary to inform that nine crimes were committed by all the business entities involved in the Brumadinho case, namely, Vale S.A. and Tüv Süd Bureau de Projetos e Consultoria LTDA. According to the Public Prosecutor's Office of the State of Minas Gerais, the crimes committed were crimes against fauna (articles 29, header and § 1, item II, and § 4, items V and VI, 33, header, Law No. 9,605/1998); crimes against flora (articles 38, header, 38-A, header, 40, header, and 48, combined with 53, item I, of Law No. 9,605/1998, which increases the penalty from one-sixth to one-third); and pollution crime (art. 54, § 2, item III, of Law No. 9,605/1998; MPMG, 2020).

In this way, it becomes possible to analyze the maximum amount that would be owed by the companies involved, in this sense, it should be noted that the fine is calculated in fine days, where the daily amount is limited to five minimum salaries, at the time of the facts, therefore five times 998 Reals, multiplied by 360, equivalent to each day, tripled, for being ineffective according to the Penal Code, three times, because it is ineffective according to the Environmental Crimes Law. Consequently, each crime would generate a pecuniary punishment of R$16,167,600.00. It so happens that in four of these infractions there would be an increase of a maximum of one third, by virtue of article 53 of Law No. 9,605/1998. Thus, the aforementioned penalty to be applied to each company is approximately R$167,065,200.00. It should be noted that this amount refers to the nine crimes in which each business entity, in the Brumadinho Case, was denounced.

Therefore, once again the disproportion that exists between the damage caused and the punishment is evident, because the latter presents itself as a small fraction of the true damage that occurred, not achieving the purpose set forth in article 59 of the CP, which states that the penalty will be established for the reprobation of the crime. In this sense, it is worth mentioning that the sum of administrative punishments is equivalent to 0.9264% of the total damage caused. The criminal sanction, in turn, which despite having a punitive bias, has the same deficiency, punishing the offender with only 0.4432% of what was estimated in relation to the total damage generated in the Brumadinho Case.

In view of this, despite a concrete Brazilian normative construction, based on philosophical, historical and evaluative aspects, the entire scenario constructed in a theoretical way is not perfected in practice. In fact, the absolute theory really has its function of existing, that is, of repaying people for the evil caused by it. It happens that, in the execution, the criminal punishment is insufficient to meet the purposes it seeks, in relation to the great environmental impacts when it comes to business entities, because the fine is less than 1% of the total value of the damage caused.

It should be noted that, according to the doctrine of prosecutor Sidnei Sá, Criminal Law aims to safeguard the most important interests, intervening only in the face of significant injuries to fundamental assets for coexistence in society. Thus, it respects the principle of minimum intervention, performing an instrumental function aimed at the effective protection of legal assets (Sá, 2006).

It happens that, despite the concrete damage to essential goods protected by the Penal Code, it cannot proportionally repay the agent for the damage caused. Thus, the fine, in the most serious cases of environmental damage, always falls short of the considerable damage caused by large companies.

It should be mentioned, as the criminology professor René Dotti clarifies, although retribution is the central idea of criminal law, it is up to it to guarantee proportionality as a phenomenon of possible equilibrium (Dotti, 1998, p. 176 and 215).

In this sense, the Absolute Theory really seeks to penalize the agent who committed an infraction in a way that is compatible with the damage caused, and there is no room to defend a sanction, at least for the absolute guideline, that is greater than the damage caused. Therefore, the penalty must be related to the harm generated, keeping proportionality with the damage proportionate, and cannot be irrelevant to the business entity, nor more expressive than the damage itself.

Finally, it is emphasized that the absolute theory emerges as an effective function of punishment with regard to the criminal liability of the business entity. However, it lacks practical improvement, considering that Criminal Law must be prepared not only to address damages of lesser and medium magnitude, but also to deal with significant environmental damage caused by large corporations.

RELATIVE THEORY AND THE LINK WITH LEGAL ENTITIES

The Relative Theory, also called Utilitarian or Preventionist, is used in the same way to justify sanctions to business entities. Thus, with regard to the functions of punishment adopted by the Penal Code in the criminal liability of the company, the relative guideline would work as a pillar to support the application of penalties in the criminal sphere.

It is worth mentioning that the German philosopher Hegel, who was one of those responsible for the emergence of the Relative Theory, sought to establish this strand in relation to the reestablishment of the broken legal order. In a concise way, the developed strand was explained by the following phrase: "punishment is the negation of the negation of the Law" (Hegel, 2009).

In this sense, still following Hegel's lessons, the origin of thought occurred with the violation of criminal legislation by a certain agent, thus generating a first negation that is that of Law. In view of this, with the denial of the right by the criminal offender, there was, therefore, a rupture of the validity of the general will, also understood as the legal order, which must be reestablished, through a new denial, a negative act aimed at curbing the previous act practiced, through a certain punishment imposed by the State (Hegel, 2009).

It turns out that the foundation of the theory developed by the aforementioned philosopher was not linked to an idea of retribution to the agent of harm caused by it, therefore, it did not seek to fight harm with another harm. It is worth mentioning that, according to Hegel, it would be illogical to desire additional damage just because there has already been a previous loss, which is what the Absolute strand asserts (Hegel, 2009).

It should be noted that the imposition of the criminal sanction has as its central objective to reestablish the legal order that had been broken through the criminal offense. Thus, in a direct analysis between the philosopher Immanuel Kant and the philosopher Georg Hegel, it is possible to extract that the latter based the construction of the theory on the legal sense, as opposed to the one that was linked to the moral sense.

In this sense, it can be emphasized that the relative theory diverges from the absolute one in the aspect of not considering punishment as an end in itself, but as a means that acts together with the social body and the individual himself, aiming to inhibit the practice of a crime. Therefore, while the absolute current seeks to apply a sanction only for having occurred a crime, the relative aspect aims at the non-practice of new crimes, with the objective of prevention.

Entering into the practical aspect of the Relative Theory, it should be noted that article 59 of the Penal Code indicates that the sanction must be necessary and sufficient for the prevention of crime, establishing the applicable amount, within the limits provided, so that the penalty applied punishes the offender and, in execution, will be used to prevent the return to criminality (Brazil, 1940).

It is worth mentioning that the Relative Theory is seen by the doctrinal scope as a genus, of which general and special prevention are species. In fact, each of these species mentioned is divided into positive and negative.

Regarding general prevention, simple terms, it would have a broader perspective, encompassing in the object of study society as a whole, which has agents capable of practicing certain criminal conduct to a criminally protected legal good. In this sense, the focus is not on the individual figure of the agent who committed a crime or who has the potential to do so, but on the community. Consequently, the entire doctrinal elaboration focuses on the social impacts resulting from the imposition of punishments.

Regarding special prevention, it is worth mentioning that it focuses on the criminal sanction that will be imposed on the active subject of the crime. Thus, the focus for such a theory is not linked to the social impact, however, it has as its main target the agent who will have a certain punishment against it. In this sense, this strand seeks the neutralization and rehabilitation of convicts.

It should be noted that the functions of sanctions not only justify Criminal Law as a whole, demonstrating that it would meet the Absolute or Relative Theory, but rather, they must be linked to each type of punishment that is possible and provided for in the national legislation. It is worth emphasizing that the fine, according to criminalist Marina Coelho Araújo, has a retributive bias, however, the other punishments that are subject to application to business entities, brought by Law 9.605/1998, namely, the penalties restrictive of rights and those of community service, these, in fact, reveal an attribute of a more preventive nature (Coelho Araújo, 2017, p. 183).

According to the Doctor of Law and professor at USP, Alamiro Velludo Salvador Netto, the restriction of rights, including the provision of services to the community, "at the core of the criminal liability of legal entities, appear as responses that are not necessarily substitutive, gaining the attribute of direct sanctions, and that obey, in most cases, prevention criteria". In this sense, according to the professor, the main objective is to promote adjustments in the business structure so that the deficiencies identified by society are corrected, resulting in the adoption of internal standards aligned with the objectives established by the State (Netto, 2018, p. 266).

Finally, it should be noted that in Brazil, in relation to Criminal Law, the Relative Strand has joint application with the Absolute Strand, having the name of Unitary or Mixed Theories. Thus, both are responsible for the functions of the sanction in criminal liability.

In view of this, we move on to the analysis of the General Positive, General Negative, Special Positive and Special Negative Preventions, tracing the link of each type with the criminal liability of the business entity.

Positive General Prevention

At first, it is known that Positive General Prevention is a kind of Relative Theory. In addition, this aspect materializes with the search for action before the occurrence of the criminal practice. In fact, with regard to the term "general", it has a reference to the objective of the present species, which aims to make the penalty become a political-criminal instrument aimed at removing each member of society from criminal activities, in a collective way. Therefore, the concept studied here has as its objective, not singular individuals, but the totality of them, which make up society.

It should be said that the method that General Positive Prevention has to inhibit members of society from committing typical facts is through trust in respect for the laws. In this way, it seeks to demonstrate to the whole society the validity of the laws and the confirmation of the legally protected values.

According to the German judge Winfried Hassemer, who defended the establishment of the penalty for preventive purposes, he asserts that the sanction would fulfill a role of ensuring the rules themselves as well as making all individuals aware of the need for the existence of each regulation, with the purpose of better coexistence (Hassemer, 2007, p. 82).

It should be clarified that, as the jurist Luiz Flávio Gomes points out, in this vein, that the objective of the criminal sphere, according to the General Positive Prevention, would not be linked, as occurs in the Absolute Theory, to the fact of causing suffering to the agent in response to the violation of the criminal law. However, support would be sought in the conception of the idea of validity, usefulness and relevance of punitive norms so that they would make it possible to live together in society (Gomes, 1999, p. 94).

The jurist and philosopher Hans Welzel complements by mentioning that the primary mission of criminal law would no longer be the current protection of legal assets, since the performance of such a branch of law would be linked to a pre-existing damage to said asset. Therefore, the jurist defends the objective "of ensuring the real validity of fundamental ethical-social values by society, overcoming a preventive-negative view", which will be analyzed in due course (Welzel, 1993, p.13).

Therefore, the core of the Theory of Positive General Prevention lies in the idea of the validity of criminal norms, demonstrating to the whole society the usefulness and relevance that exists in the law, to enable people to live together. Thus, for the present aspect, the real maintenance of the ethical and social values of society must be ensured.

Therefore, in fact, Positive General Prevention seeks to prevent future crimes in society, through the awareness of the population in an integral way, not through intimidating approaches, but by reaffirming the validity of the legal system, imposing penalties on those who transgress it.

It should be mentioned that the German jurist, Claus Roxin, asserts that positive general prevention has three purposes, namely, "the learning effect, socio-pedagogically motivated, the exercise of confidence in the right that originates in the population through the activity of criminal justice" and that of pacification, which is produced when the general legal conscience is reassured by the sanction applied to the perpetrator of the crime (Roxin, 1997, p. 91-92).

In fact, the professor at the University of Barcelona, Santiago Mir Puig, reinforces these intrinsic purposes of the theory, mentioning that they are the following: "informative function, whose objective is to inform citizens what should and should not be done; a second function related to trust, to strengthen the credibility of the legal system; finally, a function of imposition, whose intention is to strengthen the respect that individuals have for positive laws" (Puig, 2007, p. 64-65).

In this sense, it can be stated that, according to the Theory of General Positive Prevention, at least in a first level of analysis, no action would be required on the part of individuals or even legal entities, since the obligation to provide confidence in the legal system would be the responsibility of the State. In this way, it would be up to the government, seeking to stimulate security in the law, to keep in full operation the activity of all criminal justice, understood as criminal investigation, procedural issues, trial, application of the law, among others. Therefore, with regard to the purpose of trust in the law and pacification, the whole society would behave in a passive way, since it would be up to the Government to act to demonstrate to all members of the community that there is efficiency of the aforementioned right.

In fact, the objective of pacification, mentioned by Claus Roxin, would be linked to the population's confidence in the activity of the criminal justice system. This is because it would be demonstrated to everyone in society that the regulations are in force and there would be confirmation of the values outlined by the legislation (Roxin, 1997).

In view of this, the correct way to educate the entire population not to commit a crime would not have its essence in the amount of punishment applied to an agent, but, according to the lessons of Claus Roxin, what will inhibit criminal conduct will be the efficiency of the Law in ensuring that each criminal conduct will be investigated, prosecuted and punished according to the law. Therefore, one should not concentrate efforts, for the present theory, on how much would be applied to threaten third parties not to commit crimes, but rather on the certainty of punishment, both for individuals and for legal entities (Roxin, 1997, p. 91-92).

In this context, it should be emphasized that business crimes manifest an intrinsic complexity. Often, the actions perpetrated by business entities are deeply intertwined in corporate strategies, accounting practices and corporate transactions, making them difficult to identify and investigate. Thus, many of the documents essential for the disclosure of the illicit act are under secrecy, protected within the legal entity, thus making it difficult to access and obtain the necessary evidence.

It should also be noted that, in environmental crimes committed by companies, the difficulty of investigation is aggravated by various factors. In some situations, the complexity lies in the fact that some environmental damage is difficult to perceive immediately or even because it manifests itself in a hidden way, such as atmospheric pollution, water contamination in some cases and oil spills in the open sea.

It should also be noted that there are environmental infractions that can be challenging due to their evident magnitude, as in the case of significant environmental disasters, such as dam failures, forest deforestation or even illegal disposal of hazardous waste, where the extent of the damage makes the investigation and assessment of impacts extremely complex. In this sense, a complete analysis must be carried out, analyzing all the complexity of the crimes, which may involve damage to fauna and flora, the pollution generated, significant impacts on local communities, loss of biodiversity, contamination of soil, groundwater and watercourses, among others.

Therefore, in the face of crimes that are difficult to perceive or even of significant damage where the activity of their delimitation will be extremely complex, the approach to these crimes requires significant efforts of regulation, effective monitoring and application of the law to guarantee the validity of the laws and the confirmation of constitutional values to the entire population.

In view of this, in the face of crimes as complex as business crimes, which may even be difficult to verify, it would be up to the Government to allocate significant financial, human and technological resources, aiming to achieve the purposes of Positive General Prevention, namely, trust in the law and pacification.

It so happens that for all that has been exposed in the theoretical panorama, it is evident the difficulty that exists in the government's quest to demonstrate the maintenance of the laws, which hinders the application of the Theory of Positive General Prevention. This is because, in view of the inherent complexity of environmental crimes, it becomes extremely difficult for the state to ensure that laws are in force, through effective punishment for each crime committed by business entities.

It should be mentioned that crimes in Criminal Law can be divided into material, formal or mere conduct crimes. With regard to material crime, it is understood as that which demands a change in the factual world for the crime to be consummated, which is considered a naturalistic result. Regarding the formal crime, it does not need the aforementioned naturalistic result for the unlawful conduct to be entirely configured. Finally, crimes of mere conduct do not require any material consequence provided for in the rule.

In this sense, it should be noted that environmental crimes that can be committed by business entities are generally considered material crimes and, in some situations, are formal. However, when analyzing in theory the infractions that would be possible if there were legislation, based on article 173, § 5, of the Federal Constitution, where there would be the criminalization of business conducts against the economic, financial and popular economy, there would be many typifications based on both the material type of crimes and the formal type of crimes. Therefore, it would tend to be even more difficult for the government to carry out any activity in the search for the demonstration of the validity of the laws, since there would be typifications that did not require the naturalistic result.

Finally, it is worth mentioning one of Roxin's lessons on the preventive effects of crimes committed by companies. The author states that "the greatest threats to legal assets originate from the action of large conglomerates of corporations", therefore, the activities of such entities must be influenced by demonstrating "the efficiency of the legal order in protecting the community" (Roxin, 1997, p. 91-92).

In view of this, it is evident the need for the efficiency of the legal order in protecting the community against business entities, since they cause the greatest environmental damage. However, it should be emphasized that this fact must be aligned with strict criteria of the legislation, as well as inspection, aiming at the prevention of crimes, so that damage to the environment is prevented. In this way, there would be the confirmation of the values of society and the validity of the norms.

It is concluded, therefore, that the General Positive Theory of the function of punishment does not have plausible compatibility of application for legal entities. This is because, given the complexity of the investigations of each business crime, some crimes are not reported and others are not analyzed in full, which contributes to unpunishability, since it lacks effective supervision and conviction.

General Negative Prevention

The Theory of Negative General Prevention has a field similar to that of the Positive General Theory, since they seek early protection from crimes, with an impact on the whole society, however, they differ in the way to achieve the objective.

For the present theory analyzed, it uses the threat that there will be effective punishment if there is an unlawful act. In this way, it is sought through intimidation to the whole society that, if there is a criminal practice, there will therefore be the appropriate punishment.

According to the German judge Winfried Hassemer, the penalty would fulfill a role of ensuring the norms themselves as well as making all individuals aware of the need for the existence of each regulation, with the purpose of better coexistence (Hassemer, 2007, p. 82).

It is also worth mentioning that, according to the German philosopher, Ludwig Feuerbach, who formulated the theory of psychological coercion, the imposition of punishment on the convicted generates, in society, a feeling of fear. In this sense, the addressees of the norm are psychologically coerced not to commit a crime. It so happens that, from this follow-up, it is possible to criticize the sense that the human being ceases to be a symbol of honor and freedom to serve as a means to achieve an end before society (Dotti, 2010, p. 422).

Thus, when intimidating itself through punishment, it should always seek to punish as severely as possible, so that there is a reinforcement of the intimidation effect. Therefore, according to the Theory of Negative General Prevention, there would be an incentive for the application of more severe sanctions, in order to serve as an example for other members of society.

In this vein, it is worth adding an old Arabic saying that says that those who fear hell naturally avoid encountering it, because it is logical to deduce that they will act appropriately, avoiding possible sinful outcomes in the journey of life. In this way, it could be extracted that, when intimidated by the penalties applied to a third party, it generates in the population a fear that it will happen in a similar way.

It should be said that, even if the objective is to threaten all individuals about the validity of the laws, the penalty cannot be excessively severe for the agents, even if it has the objective of coercion, because the fundamental rights of each member of society must be ensured, especially the dignity of the human person and, in the case of business, that of the preservation of society. Therefore, the coercion that the norm must apply so that there are no new future crimes cannot, under any circumstances, neglect the values set forth in the Federal Constitution.

It is of paramount importance to mention the teachings of the German jurist Paul Anselm von Feuerbach, who systematized the theory of general prevention in the idea of "psychological intimidation". In this way, the penalty would act through coercion, materialized by the State. Consequently, for the present guideline, there would be a search for an excessively relevant counter motive that could distance the whole society from criminal practice (Feuerbach, 1989, p. 57-64).

It turns out that a business entity itself could not be punished by the bias of psychological intimidation, since it would lack a bio-sociological element capable of creating in the corporate entity itself the awareness of the coercion that the norm seeks to generate. In this way, due to the aforementioned lack of capacity, considering that the company is an abstract being, it could not be the target of threats by the Criminal Law, only its representatives.

On this subject, Prosecutor João Araújo Júnior adds that, in view of the Theory of Negative General Prevention, companies cannot be intimidated because, "the penalties would not exert any inhibiting effect on them, as they do not have a conscience on which the fear of sanction could act". It should also be said that in view of the interpersonal character of the moral entity, it would not be possible to have forms of intimidation against it (Araújo Júnior, 1999, p. 93).

However, the representatives of the business entity could be targets of the aforementioned intimidation, causing the entire entity not to carry out certain criminal conduct. Thus, by ignoring the figure of the company, since it is unable to understand the coercions so that a certain illegal conduct is not carried out, its representatives are punished, who reveal the necessary elements to understand the validity of the laws and the aforementioned intimidation in not committing crimes through the business entity.

In view of this, the Theory of Negative General Prevention, which has peaceful application with regard to the individual, since it threatens a certain individual who will be the target of a specific penalty, in relation to the business entity, it is worth pointing out that the application would take place in a different way, but that in no way would it harm its purpose, as it intimidates the representatives of the aforementioned entity, but, if non-compliance occurs, he is responsible for the sanctions. Thus, the coercion falls on a different subject so that, in the interest of a third party, he does not practice a criminal action, at the risk that, in case of practice, society will respond to criminal law.

Another situation that should be mentioned about the Theory of Negative General Prevention concerns punishment as a potential intimidation. The punishment to be imposed on the business entity, to avoid the practice of infractions, must be sufficiently capable of discouraging criminal conduct. Therefore, it is necessary to analyze the possible sanctions with regard to the criminal liability of the company, in view of the preventive purpose.

In this sense, it should be noted that each sanction provided for by law must exude the purpose it seeks. This is because the functions in criminal liability do not aim to justify the application of any punishment, but rather, seek that each one has in its core an intention corresponding to at least one objective adopted by the punitive legislation, which are, Absolute and Relative Theory. Therefore, these purposes must be linked to each type of penalty that is possible and provided for in the national legislation.

It is worth mentioning that, when analyzing individuals, they can be sentenced to custodial sentences, which serves the function of retribution and prevention, but in relation to companies, these can only be, according to Law 9.605/1998, article 21, contented to pay a fine, to have their rights restricted and to provide services to the community. Thus, when disregarding the deprivation of liberty, which would meet the preventive criterion of society, due to physical impossibility, one must consider which of the possible sanctions can achieve such a purpose.

Regarding the fine, its predominantly compensatory nature, seeking to sanction the agent according to the seriousness of the infraction committed. In this sense, pecuniary punishment would be essential to repay the evil done by the agent to himself, thus meeting the Absolute Theory of the function of punishment, however, it would not serve a preventive purpose.

With regard to the restriction of rights and service to the community, which are provided for in Law 9.605/1998, these, in fact, reveal an attribute of a preventive nature. In this way, the aforementioned criminal sanctions would not be directly linked to the Absolute Theory of the Function of the Penalty, however, they would be linked to the Relative guideline, as clarified by criminal lawyer Marina Coelho Araújo (Coelho Araújo, 2017, p. 183).

At first, regarding the provision of services to the community by the business entity, this, according to Law 9.605/1998, art. 23, will consist of: "funding of environmental programs and projects; execution of works to recover degraded areas; maintenance of public spaces; contributions to public environmental or cultural entities" (Brazil, 1998, p. 3).

In this sense, it is worth mentioning that the punishments provided for the provision of services to the community are considered to be below, in a comparative way, the prison sentence in relation to individuals. This is because the provision of services to the community would not delimit in any way the company's performance in relation to the activity itself. Therefore, when analyzing how the business entity would handle each sanction, it should disburse a certain amount to meet a public need and perhaps deploy outsourced personnel to meet the penalties.

From another perspective, the penalties restricting the company's rights, according to Law 9.605/1998, article 22, are: partial or total suspension of activities; temporary interdiction of establishment, work or activity; and prohibition of contracting with the Government, as well as obtaining subsidies, subsidies or donations from it (Brazil, 1998, p. 3).

Regarding the aforementioned restrictions on the rights of the company, unlike the provision of services to the community, it is comparable to the penalty of deprivation of liberty imposed on the individual. This is because, by suspending activities, prohibiting establishments, works or activities and prohibiting the hiring, obtaining of subsidies, subsidies or donations with the Government, it ends up directly interfering in the business flow, which generates a significant shock to society capable of preventing future illegal acts, in light of the deprivation of liberty for individuals.

Therefore, it is concluded that the sanctions provided for in the criminal legislation have, in fact, a threatening character towards the business entity, making it feel coerced not to commit a crime, thus meeting the character of the General Negative Prevention of the function of the penalty.

Finally, it should be noted that the Theory of Negative General Prevention suffers specific criticism from the doctrine, as pointed out by the University of Chicago economist, Gary Becker, with regard to individuals, this is because most people when they plan to carry out a criminal action, in fact, do not perform such precise mathematical calculations to know whether or not a certain crime is worth being executed. It is not denied that the penalty, in the case of imprisonment, has an intimidating power, but the natural agents often act ignoring the evil that will be contracted, which goes beyond the criminal act practiced (Becker, 1974).

In this sense, it should be noted that, unlike what occurs with individuals, companies have a more accurate character, through calculations, it would be possible, through rational means, to determine the best action to be taken by the business entity. That is, societies will generally consider calculations on the amount they will need to act in a way that does not harm the environment and sums of how much savings there will be if they harm nature, with possible sanctions.

From this scenario, it should be said that, for the present theory, these calculations are positive, since it is expected that, when analyzing the potential penalties, all legal entities, based on the aforementioned calculations, will deviate from practices harmful to Criminal Law and opt for non-criminal conducts. This is because it will be a more cost-effective conduct for business entities to follow criminal legislation, since the risks associated with criminal practice did not compensate for the potential gains of crime.

Therefore, it is concluded that there is compatibility between the Theory of General Negative Prevention and legal entities. This is because there are preventive penalties that have an intimidating effect capable of interfering in the business flow of the business entity. Only the conflict concerning the subjects subject to threat and those subject to liability in any criminal practice is highlighted, which reveal themselves as distinct subjects.

Special Positive Prevention

When dealing with Special Positive Prevention, it is worth mentioning that it was constructed with the aim of a function of punishment directed to the future, that is, it aims to prevent crimes from occurring. In addition, the special aspect concentrates the purpose of the sanction on the agent who committed a crime, in this sense, it should be clarified that the present modality analyzed seeks to encourage the readaptation of the agent himself in society.

According to the doctor and professor in Criminal Law, Déa Carla Nery, positive special prevention materializes in the search for the resocialization of the offender. It is noteworthy that the present theory aims at the reinsertion of the transgressor into society, through correction (Nery, 2005).

It should be said, as the professor clarifies, that the punishment is directed at the treatment of the agent itself, with the aim of focusing on his personality, with the objective of avoiding a possible recurrence. In this way, the sanction defended by the Special Positive Prevention has a purpose of penalty-treatment, which flows into the rehabilitation itself (Nery, 2005).

It should be mentioned that, according to the lessons of the German jurist Hassemer, punishment only becomes legitimate when it has the capacity to promote the rehabilitation of the criminal. In this sense, it should be noted that, with the full fulfillment of the punishment or with the obtaining of conditional release, if the legal requirements are present, the agent must return to social life prepared to respect the rules imposed on everyone by the Law, since there was a concern with the rehabilitation of the convicted person (Hassemer, 2011, p. 543).

Therefore, it is worth noting that this function of the penalty considers that the crime has already occurred, being successful in the inspection, in the progress of the process and in the effective conviction of the agent who has not complied with the law. Therefore, the criminal agent is a person who is not adapted to social life, so he needs to be removed from it and put on rehabilitation techniques so that he can be reinserted into the social environment.

On this fact, it should be said that, according to lawyer Rafael Pelizzaro da Silveira, "by committing the crime, the individual demonstrates his deficiency in understanding the validity of the rules and, in this way, it is necessary to teach him how to live peacefully among his peers, respecting the democratically instituted legal precepts" (Silveira, 2017, p. 118).

It is worth mentioning that the Penal Execution Law, Law 7.210/84, in its article 1, asserts that the effectiveness of the sanction aims to provide conditions for the harmonious social integration of the convicted and the interned. It should be noted that the purpose dealt with by this law concerns the function of rehabilitation that must be found in punishment. It so happens that the aforementioned purpose does not differ in any way from the Theory of Special Positive Prevention and should be understood as similar (Brazil, 1984, p. 1).

At this point, it is worth noting that there are two problems to be solved, when dealing with the criminal liability of the legal entity, the first consists of the fact that the punishments provided for by legislation are, in theory, capable of ensuring a resocializing purpose to the business entity, while the second is about whether said corporate entity can be reinstated. Therefore, it is necessary to analyze both the sanction and the society itself, in the light of the Theory of Special Positive Prevention, in order to determine whether it would be possible to apply the end of social re-education to companies.

Regarding the penalties that are inherent to the business entity, it is worth remembering that not all of them serve the preventive purpose. Regarding the fine, this, according to the doctrine, supported by the doctor of law and professor at USP, Alamiro Velludo Salvador Netto, has a retributive bias, aiming to punish the agent in proportion to the seriousness of the offense committed. However, regarding the other sanctioning species brought by Law 9,605/1998, namely, the restriction of rights and the provision of services to the community, these, in fact, reveal an attribute of a preventive nature, as the aforementioned professor clarifies (Netto, 2018, p. 266).

Thus, it is imperative to highlight that the analysis of the rehabilitation of the offender will occur from the restriction of the right and the provision of services to the community, since these have in their core the purpose of preventing the agent from committing new damages to society after his reintegration. Thus, the sentence must be able to resocialize the agent after involvement in illicit practices. In addition, sanctions also need to carry the objective of rebuilding the company's image in the market and in society.

At the outset, it can be highlighted that the penalties restricting the rights of the business entity, according to Law 9.605/1998, article 22, are: "partial or total suspension of activities; temporary interdiction of establishment, work or activity; and prohibition of contracting with the Public Power, as well as obtaining subsidies, subsidies or donations from it" (Brazil, 1998, p. 3).

Therefore, regarding the ways of punishing the agent by applying a kind of restriction of rights, it should be pointed out that none of them seeks to bring the convicted agent closer to the society that was a victim of environmental damage, nor any technique for the rehabilitation of the offender. This is because, by suspending activities, prohibiting establishments, works or activities and prohibiting the hiring, obtaining of subsidies, subsidies or donations with the Government, it ends up directly interfering in the business flow, causing a situation analogous to the extirpation of society from the common environment, even if it is temporary.

On the other hand, it is worth highlighting the penalty of providing services to the community by the business entity, which, according to Law 9.605/1998, art. 23, will consist of: "funding of environmental programs and projects; execution of works to recover degraded areas; maintenance of public spaces; contributions to public environmental or cultural entities" (Brazil, 1998, p. 3).

By analyzing the types of services provided to the community, it can be extracted that they are strategies adopted to repair damage caused and strengthen ties with society. This is because there would be a reconstruction of the company's image in the market and in society itself. Rehabilitation, in light of the penalties outlined in article 23 of Law 9,605/1998, therefore, is not limited to sanctions, but seeks to correct conduct, ensuring that the business entity contributes constructively to society and avoids resorting to illicit practices in the future.

It is interesting to mention that rehabilitation in the context of the criminal liability of the business entity has a significant focus on rebuilding the corporate image for the community through various forms of funding in environmental areas or in public spaces.

It so happens that the entire legislative focus operated in the external field of society, not concentrating any norm in its internal regulations, seeking to stimulate a positive change in the organizational processes of the corporate entity itself.

Therefore, it is worth mentioning that, by aiming to rehabilitate the conduct of society, it could include incentives in the legislation to adopt compliance programs, ethical training and measures to ensure that it behaves in a legal and socially responsible manner. In this way, not only the external framework of society would be affected, but also the internal one, so that it generates future repercussions, thus preventing possible damages.

In this way, by encouraging society to adopt, after committing a crime, practices and values that avoid the repetition of illegal conducts, the entire business framework would be stricter so that there would be the approval of any decision that would make the entity be the target of criminal liability again in the future.

At this point, it is worth informing that rehabilitation is understood as a right of the convict, not an obligation. Therefore, the measures of rehabilitation, reintegration and reintegration of the offender should be offered as optional to the sentenced agent. This is because the objective is to promote positive changes in the criminal's behavior, to adapt to the social body, in this way it would require a consent of the culprit itself to be re-educated to live in the community.

According to Doctor of Law Bruno de Moraes Ribeiro, the Penal Execution Law establishes that rehabilitation is a right of the convict, granting him the option to participate or not in treatment programs. According to the Doctor, the approach must respect the individuality and moral integrity of the individual, based on the adoption, by the Federal Constitution, of the principle of humanity (Ribeiro, 2008).

In the scenario of the individual, in relation to the agent's rehabilitation measures, it can be mentioned that it seeks to understand the reasons that led the agent to commit a certain criminal offense, so that the opportunity for transformation can be offered. In this sense, the right to visitation is highlighted, to bring the convict closer to relatives or friends, the right to work or study, for educational and productive purposes, and the right, in some cases, to be transferred from a certain penitentiary to another that is in a place where the sentenced person has roots, aiming at assistance from family members.

However, in relation to business entities, the techniques of approximation of the entity to society are imposed by Criminal Law, through a duty to provide services to the community. Consequently, when a sanction of services is applied to the community, it could reflect to society a false resocialization on the part of society, since it would be acting not so that it could have a new image before the social body and to attract the public's trust, but because such a practice had been imposed on the collectivity.

Thus, despite the visualization of a possible external conduct that is positive on the part of the company, there would still be no non-resocialized administrative body, which would not generate a preventive purpose, thus avoiding new crimes.

Therefore, there should, as is the case with individuals, have legislative measures encouraging social alignment with legislative norms, characterizing the right to resocialize. In addition, it is worth mentioning that the options provided by the legislation are, in fact, very restricted, based only on the external scenario of society, and there is no rule that seeks a structural change of the business entity to achieve reintegration, as is the case of compliance programs, ethical training and corporate measures to comply with laws and regulations.

It should be noted that, according to the Prosecutor João Marcelo Junior, the traditional doctrine does not admit the resocializing effect on legal entities, since the penal execution would not have the means to provide the reintegration of such entities into harmonious social life (Araújo Junior, 1999, p. 93).

In this context, it is worth mentioning that in fact the legislation in the scenario in which it finds itself, offers few possibilities to the company to be resocialized, in order to prevent new crimes. However, it is added that there are means, such as compliance, which can ensure the rehabilitation of the business entity.

Finally, it is worth criticizing the recidivism of the business entity, which seeks to prevent the event through Special Positive Prevention. It should be emphasized that, according to the Principle of Personality of the Penalty, any corporate operation that involves the reorganization of the company directly influences the criminal liability of corporate entities. Thus, business reorganization that includes the merger, incorporation or spin-off, results in the extinction of the pre-existing corporate legal personality, to form a new personality, which is dissociated from the crimes that were carried out by the previous company. This is the understanding of the current Third Section of the STJ, which asserts that the capacity of the business entity to respond to a lawsuit is not transferred with incorporation.

It turns out that it is worth considering the scenario in which all the components of the company that were involved in the decision to commit a crime against the environment were replaced. Therefore, society, seeking to bring reliability to the market and society, could replace all the people involved in the decision that generated an unlawful act. In this way, the entire corporate body that was responsible for deliberating on the commission of a crime, and with the new managers, there would be a complete change, comparable to what occurs in corporate transactions.

Therefore, in view of the parity of the situations exposed, in the light of the Principle of Personality of the Penalty, it would be possible to consider, in theory, that the company would no longer be titled as a repeat offender or with a bad criminal record, since, in fact, there would be a change in the personality of the business entity.

It is concluded that the forms exposed in the legislation that are linked to the function of rehabilitation, despite being provided for as penalties, where the agent will have a duty to comply and not a right, as in relation to individuals, it is possible to say that there is a reintegrative character to business entities. However, it is worth mentioning that, as mentioned, the legislation can advance not only with the rehabilitation of the offender, not only in the external scenario of society, but also in the internal plan of the company, e.g., with the compliance program.

Special Negative Prevention

The last form of purpose of the sentence to be analyzed concerns the Special Negative Prevention. Like the positive aspect, it aims to reach individually all people who have been convicted of a crime. In addition, it aims to ensure that the aforementioned agents do not commit new crimes, materializing the aspect of inhibition of unlawful acts.

Regarding the negative type of special prevention, its main objective is the neutralization of the agent who committed a crime. Through this modality, the offender is removed from the social life to which he belongs so that he is unable to commit new crimes.

According to lawyer Rafael Pelizzaro da Silveira, the "active subject of crime is seen as a being disqualified to integrate the community and, consequently, must be segregated so that others do not suffer from their dangerous actions" (Silveira, 2017, p. 117).

In fact, according to the professor at the University of Barcelona, Santiago Mir Puig, the negative bias of Special Prevention "is seen as a direct instrument to fight crime, always aiming at the protection of legal assets". In fact, according to the author, the purpose of applying the "legal norm is to directly confront the actions of those who commit crimes, in order to neutralize them and prevent criminal behavior from spreading in the social sphere" (Puig, 2007, p. 68).

In this way, by restricting the offender from social life, ensuring that he will have his freedom restricted, consequently, the purpose of crime prevention is achieved. This is because, a person deprived of his right to come and go, in theory, cannot put other goods essential to the right at risk of damage.

It is worth mentioning the teachings of the jurist and philosopher Cesare Beccaria, who asserts that, with regard to the "preventive function of punishment, its purpose is not to cause pain, torturing and afflicting the person, nor to undo the crime that has already been committed". In fact, the philosopher concludes that the purpose of punishment "is to prevent the guilty from committing a crime again", removing the guilty from the world of crime (Beccaria, 2014, p. 45).

It should be added that the technique brought by the Theory of Special Negative Prevention is directly related to the attempt to thwart recidivism, as warned by the doctor and professor in Criminal Law, Déa Carla Nery, who asserts that there is a search for both intimidation, for those who suffer intimidation, and deprivation of liberty, for those who are not correctable or intimidated. Therefore, according to the doctor, the objective of this guideline is to neutralize the possible new criminal action, of the one who committed the crime at a previous time. Thus, its purpose is to prevent a new commission of an illegal act through effective techniques such as isolation (Nery, 2005).

In the same way, the German jurist, Claus Roxin, explains that according to the Theory of Special Negative Prevention, there would be intimidation when possible to correct those correctable offenders, thus intimidating those who are still intimidated and subjecting to prison those who were neither correctable nor intimidable (Roxin, 1976, p.15).

However, when one wants to intimidate the intimidating or wants to neutralize those who are not, one cannot fail to mention the topic of the scope of the punitive power of the State. This is limited based on several principles, mainly the dignity of the human person and, for societies, the preservation of the company.

When analyzing the present theory in comparison with society, it is worth mentioning that, as it is an abstract being, it would not be possible for the company to be subject to incarceration, in the way conducted with individuals, due to full physical incompatibility. In fact, according to criminologist Juarez Cirino dos Santos, complete neutralization, similar to the approach of Criminal Law against individuals, would only be achievable through the closure of corporate transactions, preventing any form of social interaction. This procedure would be comparable to the imposition of the death penalty, something that has already been considered inadmissible in a democratic state (Santos, 2010, p. 281).

In this sense, it is worth reinforcing that not all penalties that are subject to application to the business entity bring the preventive aspect, such as the fine, which has a merely retributive character. In this sense, it should be noted that sanctions restricting rights and those of community service reveal an attribute of a preventive nature, as clarified by the doctor of law and professor at USP, Alamiro Velludo Salvador Netto (Netto, 2018, p. 266).

Regarding the penalty of providing services to the community by the legal entity, among the hypotheses provided for by law, whether for funding environmental projects or environmental entities, or for works to recover degraded areas or maintain public spaces, there is no room to address a possible neutralization of the corporate entity itself so that it would be prevented from practicing new criminal acts.

However, through the sanctions restricting rights applied to the company, there could be a partial or total suspension of operations, the temporary interdiction of establishments, works or activities, or the prohibition of contracting with the Government, in addition to the impossibility of receiving subsidies, subsidies or donations. Thus, when analyzing the suspension of activities and the temporary interdiction, in fact, a situation similar to the deprivation of liberty for the natural person is noted, since the neutralization would occur in a controlled manner and could be undone in the future.

In addition, the suspension of activities and the temporary interdiction would help against legal entities that are not correctable or intimidated. In this way, the neutralization of the possible new criminal action was prevented, so that the criminal behavior does not propagate in the social sphere.

Therefore, even though physical imprisonment is impossible to apply to companies, as defended by criminologist Juarez Cirino dos Santos, in view of the physical impossibility, penalties could be used that have effects similar to the restriction of the right to come and go of individuals. In this sense, the suspension of activities would generate the interruption of operations, directly impacting the company's ability to conduct normal work. Regarding the temporary interdiction, there would be a prohibition on the corporation from carrying out certain activities for a specific period. Therefore, through the application of one of the two measures mentioned, there would be prevention, through the neutralization of the business entity, in practicing criminal activities.

It is worth mentioning that, regarding the imprisonment of the individual, it only generates the impossibility of exercising freedom, not interfering in other aspects of life, such as the patrimonial aspect, which can be relocated through power of attorney, for example. With regard to the company, if there was a suspension of its activities and it could not act in any way, the punishment would go far beyond the simple restriction of freedom, because it would prevent negotiation operations, employees, circulation of goods and services, among others, which can generate a picture of state terror. Thus, it is important that the terms and conditions of the suspension or interdiction are described, so that it does not penalize more than what the Theory of Special Negative Prevention preaches.

It should be added that the lawyer Rafael Pelizzaro da Silveira mentions, in relation to the special negative prevention, that the penalty of suspension of activities, for business entities, has the power to remove the aforementioned entity from social life, causing the neutralization of actions that may harm the legal assets essential to society (Silveira, 2017, p. 126).

As for the penalty of forced liquidation, it applies in cases where the company is constituted or used, mainly, with the purpose of allowing, facilitating or concealing the practice of crimes, although it really totally prevents any recurrence from occurring, it does not have a preventive character, since the purpose of special negative prevention is to restrict the rights of the agent, to make it neutralized, with the possibility of reestablishing the status quo, but not eliminating from existence both the individual and the business entity. Such a measure of forced liquidation reflects a specific punishment for an extreme situation.

It is concluded, therefore, that the Theory of Special Negative Prevention of the function of punishment is compatible with business entities. Bearing in mind that, although the deprivation of liberty is not applicable to business entities, there are sanctions, with a preventive nature, that generate the desired effect of this aspect, that is, the neutralization of the company.

EVOLUTION AND PRACTICAL IMPLICATIONS OF THE FUNCTIONS OF PUNISHMENT

At the outset, regarding the evolution and practical implications of the functions of punishment, it is worth mentioning that the purposes of criminal sanction and the respective proposals to adapt each one to a more effective criminal responsibility will be objectively addressed, in view of the objectives of article 59 of the CP, which ensures that punishment will be determined according to what is considered necessary and sufficient to disapprove and prevent crime.

In this scenario, it is worth mentioning that the case of Brumadinho had a Parliamentary Commission of Inquiry (CPI) moved against it, to investigate the causes, identify responsibilities, investigate failures in the inspection and prevention systems and propose measures to prevent similar events from occurring in the future.

From the aforementioned CPI, it was demonstrated that, despite several statements to the press that there was nothing abnormal with the dam, the B1 dam that had been ruptured, in fact, presented substantial evidence that indicated that the entire structure had multiple problems that would justify the activation of the Emergency Action Plan for Dams (Paebm). It turns out that Vale, as well as the companies related to the fact, chose not to do so, masking information and manipulating stability data, even though they were aware of the imminent risk to human lives (Brazil CPI Parliamentary Investigative Committee Report, 2019, p. 239).

In addition, it was found that dam B1 represented only one in the middle of ten Vale tailings dams that were classified as "Attention Zone" or "ALARP Zone". With regard to this area of attention, it represents a potential probabilistic risk of rupture and demonstrates that there could be financial consequences (Brazil CPI Parliamentary Investigative Committee Report, p. 239).

It should be noted that the evidence suggests that Vale's employees could and should have taken steps to avoid the tragic outcome, but chose not to act. It should be noted that everyone was aware of the imminent risk of B1 dam failure, however, no effort was made to prevent the dam from breaking (Brazil CPI Parliamentary Investigative Committee Report, p. 620).

In this sense, it is imperative to highlight that, with the previous information about the substantial damages that could exist, there was still an assessment of the costs of living for the purpose of compensation, repair actions, restructuring, environmental shocks, among others, and it was decided that paying compensation, instead of preventing environmental crime, would be more beneficial to Vale from a financial point of view.

Therefore, the Criminal Law failed to ensure a complete punishment to the companies involved, not assertively applying the purposes of the sanction, that is, retribution and prevention, so that no crime would even be considered by large corporations. This is because, if there is an option for damage, it is the main legal assets of society that are put in danger, for the benefit of the corporate entity.

It is not an excessive punishment, without any basis, punishing the business entity only for being able to profit too much, but rather, it seeks to enforce the precepts set forth in article 59 of the Penal Code, so that the punishment causes reprobation and prevention of crime. Therefore, it is essential to establish a legal framework that enables the imposition of strict penalties, which have more forceful financial, restrictive, and preventive implications, which leads to an effective punitive system.

Regarding the Absolute Theory, it is essential to point out that it emerges as an effective function of punishment with regard to the criminal liability of the business entity. In this sense, it should be said again that its role is exclusively punitive, seeking to apply to the agent damages proportional to the crime he committed. However, as for the practical component of the absolute guideline, there is insufficiency in dealing with large companies and, therefore, needs improvement, since the skillful preparation is related to small and medium-sized corporations.

On the present subject, the doctrine, as mentioned by criminalist Marina Coelho Araújo, maintains that the only penalty that can be applied against legal entities, which exude the punitive character, are fines. In fact, with regard to this aspect, not only criminal liability can be presented as a pecuniary punishment in the specific case, but also the environmental administrative sanction, which also has the character of punishment (Coelho Araújo, 2017, p. 183).

At the outset, it is worth remembering that the Samarco Case generated a damage of 47.6 billion Reals, which represents a scenario only of compensation, with no cost being accounted for as punishment, which is the responsibility of administrative and criminal justice.

In this scenario, it should be emphasized that the administrative fine is limited to 50 million Reals for each infraction, while the penalty in the criminal process can reach, in the case of Mariana, the amount of R$12,765,600.00 per crime. In fact, in the concrete situation, the administrative sanction reached the amount of 250 million, only for the direct impacts resulting from the collapse of the dam, totaling five infraction notices, it happens that other infractions were committed, reaching the sum of 20 infraction notices and the amount of 350.7 million Reals. In addition, regarding the criminal pecuniary punishment, 10 crimes were imputed to the mining company Samarco, which reveals the amount of R$127,656,000.00.

In practical terms, 350.7 million Reals, referring to infraction notices, represent approximately 0.738% of 47.6 billion Reals, while R$127,656,000.00, related to crimes committed by the business entity, represent approximately

0.2684% of the estimated damage that was caused, which would be the amount of 47.6 billion Reals.

Thus, when analyzing the effectiveness of the fines imposed, which aim to punish the agent who broke the law, it reaches about 1% (0.738% + 0.2684%) of what was actually attributed to the damage caused.

In order to improve the current approach to the Absolute Theory in the legal sphere, it is proposed to consider and implement adjustments aimed at the typification of new conducts, as well as the readjustment of criminal fines when it comes to crimes committed by business entities.

On this aspect, Bill (PL) No. 2,787/2019 seeks to implement new typical conducts for the punishment of companies. The aforementioned bill aims to amend the Environmental Crimes Law to add two new typifications of criminal conducts, the first would be that of "causing an ecological disaster by atmospheric, water or soil contamination, by the significant destruction of flora or death of animals, which generates a state of public calamity", which would be known as the crime of ecocide, and the second typification would be that of "causing a dam rupture due to non-compliance with the legislation, technical standard, license and its conditions or determination of the environmental authority and the dam safety inspection entity" (Brazil, 2019, p. 601).

Regarding the readjustment of criminal fines, when it comes to crimes committed by business entities, this is a subject that is not yet highlighted in the Chamber of Deputies or the Federal Senate, but it should be noted that the aforementioned Bill No. 2,787/2019 also aims to increase environmental administrative pecuniary punishments to values between a minimum of two thousand Reals and a maximum of one billion Reals (Brazil, 2019).

Therefore, by implementing new typifications as well as raising the maximum amount that legal agents can be held criminally liable, it will make the criminal punishment fair, considering that it may be proportional to the real value of the damage caused to society and, therefore, will effectively repay the agent for the damage caused by it, making the Absolute Theory have a perfect effect in the practical aspect.

Another aspect that demands analysis falls on the sphere of the Theory of Positive General Prevention, which deals with the influence of society on respect for the laws. This guideline uses aspects of trust in respect for laws, validity of norms and even confirmation of society's values.

As previously mentioned, business crimes have an inherent complexity to them, some crimes are not reported and many others are not analyzed in full, which contributes to unpunishability, since it lacks inspection and monitoring, to confirm the values of society and the validity of the rules and, in this way, prevent crimes.

It is known that, in recent decades, there have been legislative increases for the inspection of mining dams, represented by Law No. 12,334/2010 and subsequent infra-legal norms, from which the National Dam Safety Policy (PNSB) is established. However, there is a certain limitation in human and material resources for effective inspection (Brazil Relatório CPI, 2019).

Furthermore, despite the transformation of the National Department of Mineral Production (DNPM) into the National Mining Agency (ANM), the administration and inspection consequences resulting from the former still persist. The Federal Court of Auditors carried out an audit in 2019 at the ANM, in order to observe a large budget and financial deficit, lack of employee training and reduced technical staff, causing a high exposure to fraud and corruption (Brazil CPI Parliamentary Investigative Committee Report, 2019).

On the other hand, there was a great evolution in the information management system of mining dams and, consequently, some improvement in inspection. This fact is due to the transformation of the body in which the data about the aforementioned fact were entered, previously done in the Annual Mining Report (RAL) and in the Integrated Mining Dam Safety Management System (SIGBM). The RAL organized such information in a spreadsheet, after inspections. However, the process could take several months, corroborating fraud in the system. From the SIGBM, a communication channel was inaugurated between entrepreneurs and the ANM, with ease in registration and structural data, allowing the visualization and verification of information in a maximum of 15 days, in order to reduce the time needed to complete the inspection (Brazil, 2019).

Thus, the legislative and infra-legal norms were modified after the Mariana tragedy and expanded after the Brumadinho disaster. Such events contributed to the improvement of the Brazilian environmental inspection system (Brazil, 2019).

In view of the above, it was found by the CPI of the Mariana Case that there really is a deficiency in several aspects, which leads to the inefficiency of the inspection of all crimes committed by legal entities. Regarding this scenario, it is worth noting that there is a need for human and material resources for effective inspection, budgeting and training of employees, so that it does not generate a high exposure to fraud and corruption.

On the other hand, it should be noted that, through the evolution of the information management system and the elaboration of general rules for the licensing of projects that impact or may impact directly or indirectly the environment, it will contribute to a more efficient inspection. It is worth mentioning that PL No. 2,785/2019, which establishes general rules for the licensing of mining enterprises, seeks the preventive purpose of the penalty, compatible with the General Positive aspect of prevention.

Therefore, it is clear that there must be more injection of resources and improvement of inspection systems in order to achieve the objective of influencing society that the laws are in force and deserve to be respected, since inspection and monitoring would be efficient, enabling a conviction in case of criminal practices. Thus, the criterion of Positive General Prevention would be met.

When analyzing the General Negative strand, it was mentioned that it seeks to dissuade society through the fear of criminal consequences. Although companies are not the target of restriction of freedom, as are individuals, they have sanctions that bring in their core the preventive purpose that can cause fear to societies, that is, those that restrict rights.

In this sense, regarding the fine, its predominantly retributive character is retributive, but in relation to the penalties of restriction of rights, these, in fact, reveal an attribute of a preventive nature, as clarified by criminal lawyer Marina Coelho Araújo (Coelho Araújo, 2017, p. 183).

These aforementioned restrictions on the rights of the business entity not only meet the preventive criterion, but can also interfere so significantly in the corporate structure of the company that it can be used as a way to coerce society not to commit crimes at the risk of responding to criminal consequences. According to Law 9.605/1998, article 22, "the penalties restricting rights are: partial or total suspension of activities; temporary interdiction of establishment, work or activity; and prohibition of contracting with the Public Power, as well as obtaining subsidies, subsidies or donations from it" (Brazil, 1998, p. 3).

Therefore, it is concluded that the penalties provided for in the criminal legislation have, in fact, a threatening character towards the legal entity, making it feel coerced not to commit a crime, thus meeting the character of the General Negative Prevention of the sanction function, not requiring any practical improvement.

Another preventive theory is the special positive one, which concerns the rehabilitation, resocialization and reintegration of the offender, promoting positive changes in the behavior of the convict, to adapt them to society.

As already mentioned in this chapter, not all criminal sanctions serve the preventive purpose, only the restrictions of law and the provision of services to the community, in fact, reveal an attribute of a preventive nature, as clarified by the Doctor of Law and professor at USP, Alamiro Velludo Salvador Netto (Netto, 2018, p. 266).

It so happens that, as mentioned in its own chapter, the penalties with a preventive nature that aim at the purpose of resocializing the offender are those of community service. According to Law 9.605/1998, article 23, the referred punishments are: "funding of environmental programs and projects; execution of works to recover degraded areas; maintenance of public spaces; contributions to public environmental or cultural entities" (Brazil, 1998, p. 3).

About these penalties, it can be mentioned that they are actually strategies adopted to repair damage caused and strengthen ties with society. This is because there would be a reconstruction of the company's image in the market and in society itself.

It turns out that the entire legislative focus operated in the external field of the company, not concentrating any norm in its internal regulations, seeking to stimulate a positive change in the organizational processes of the corporate entity itself. It can encourage the use of compliance programs, ethical training, and measures to ensure that society behaves in a legal and socially responsible manner.

In this sense, it is worth mentioning that, regarding compliance, it is provided for in the legislation, in Federal Decree No. 11,129/2022, with the following main objectives: "to prevent, detect, and remedy deviations, fraud, irregularities, and unlawful acts practiced against the public administration, national or foreign; and foster and maintain a culture of integrity in the organizational environment" (Brazil, 2022, p. 14).

Still on this subject, it should be noted that the company's internal environment, for the establishment of compliance, needs some requirements, such as the commitment of senior management, for efficient management, accountability, risk analysis, which must be a recurring practice in society to prevent future damages, the elaboration of a code of conduct, the internal investigation, which may use inspectors in the legal entity to perform this function, and the whistleblowing program, which is understood as a form of anonymous complaints to correct various conducts. Finally, it is worth mentioning that, in the event of behavioral deviations, disciplinary measures would be applied against those involved.

In this way, it is concluded that it is not only possible to make an external change, seeking the resocialization of the company, however, it is possible, in the face of various methods, to implement systems in the business entity itself so that it demonstrates the rehabilitation of the offender. In this way, a corporate entity, in fact, can be reintegrated into society, aiming at a better coexistence.

Thus, by adopting measures such as compliance, future environmental problems could be prevented, for example. There will even be an improvement in the company's reputation before society and the market.

In this way, there could be in the legislation, in order to rehabilitate the offender, not only rules that deal with the external aspect of the company, but also with the internal scenario, aiming to really promote a change in behavior in the convicted, to adapt them to society.

Another problem to be mentioned concerns whether it is a right or a duty to rehabilitate the offender. Based on the entire scenario of criminal liability of the individual, reintegration is understood as a simple option of the convicted, in addition, it is always provided with various incentives to encourage them to qualify for living in society.

In this scenario, one can cite Law No. 7,210/1984, article 126, which allows the convict who serves their sentence in a closed or semi-open regime the power to redeem, by work or study, part of the time of execution of the punishment. It is also added that, in the first paragraph of the aforementioned article, the time count referred to in the header will be made at the rate of one day of sanction for every 12 hours of school attendance, divided into at least three days and one day of punishment for every three days of work (Brazil, 1984, p. 24).

In this way, it was demonstrated that, through the incentives, it is possible to have an ex-convict who has been rehabilitated to live in society, which is promising for the whole society and market. About this, it is mentioned that the objective is to promote positive changes in the criminal's behavior, to adapt to the social body, in this way they would need the consent of the culprit himself to be re-educated to live in community.

In this sense, Doctor of Law Bruno de Moraes Ribeiro, the Penal Execution Law establishes that rehabilitation is a right of the convict, granting him the option of participating or not in treatment programs. According to the

Doctor, the approach must respect the individuality and moral integrity of the individual, based on the adoption, by the Federal Constitution, of the principle of humanity (Ribeiro, 2008).

It can be mentioned that, by imposing a conduct on the convicted person to act in a way that would be the result of a rehabilitation process, it ends up masking all members of society and the market that there was a false rehabilitation of the offender, since he did not choose to perform a service to the community, but this action was imposed on him. Furthermore, such an attitude does not tend to generate a positive change in the behavior of the sentenced, since, it is reinforced, the choice for reintegration did not come from the delinquent.

Finally, regarding the Special Negative Prevention, it is worth pointing out that the rules that deal with the recurrence of the company, which is what the theory seeks to avoid, need legislative improvement, so that it can cover situations that would not be possible when it comes to the individual. An example is the case in which all the components of society that were responsible for the commission of the crime were replaced, thus questioning whether it would still be necessary, according to the entire legal and principled system, to title as a repeat offender or possessing a bad criminal record the corporation that adopts such practice.

Regarding Special Negative Prevention, this theory asserts that the penalty should be applied to avoid new criminal practices by the offender, in this sense, it would be necessary to physically neutralize the agent. Some authors maintain that this measure could be a response to the present aspect, but it could also be just a simple intimidation for the agents who are still intimidated.

In this sense, as previously pointed out, the preventive purpose of the sanction is only found in the provision of service to the community and in the restriction of rights. In the latter, there are, in fact, effective forms of neutralization, as stated in article 22 of the Environmental Crimes Law, through the "partial or total suspension of activities, temporary interdiction of establishment, work or activity or prohibition of contracting with the

Public Power, as well as obtaining subsidies, subsidies or donations from it". Thus, when analyzing both the suspension of activities and the temporary interdiction, in fact, a situation similar to the sanction of deprivation of liberty for the individual is noted, since the aforementioned impediment would occur in a controlled manner and could be undone in the future (Brazil, 1998, p. 3).

Thus, when analyzing the Theory of Special Negative Prevention, it does not need practical evolutions and improvements in its application as a function of the penalty. In addition, it is perfectly applicable in the context of legal entities. Bearing in mind that, although the deprivation of liberty is not applicable to legal entities, there are sanctions, with a preventive nature, that can generate the desired effect of this aspect, that is, the neutralization of the company.

In summary, although the functions of punishment have an intrinsic compatibility with business entities, it should be noted that there are few cases of these purposes of punishment that do not require practical improvements. Thus, challenges remain that require substantial practical changes to evolve and implement. The effective application of the aforementioned purposes to companies requires continuous review and improvements in the normative framework and legal practices. The search for the effectiveness and adequacy of corporate sanctions remains a constant journey, especially in relation to the fact of inspection, aiming to more effectively achieve the fundamental purposes of punishments in the context of legal entities. Understanding these nuances is crucial to guide future reflections and reforms that strengthen the punitive system in the treatment of societies, aligning itself more effectively with sanctioning objectives.

SUPREME COURTS AND INTERNATIONAL JURISPRUDENCE

After studying the theoretical foundation that structures the criminal liability of the corporate entity in the Brazilian legal system, as well as the functions of the penalty and its relationship with the business entity, it is also necessary to pragmatic study the previous chapters.

In this sense, this chapter aims to explore the decisions of the Brazilian higher courts, including, the theme of double imputation, all these topics in relation to the functions of the penalty with regard to the corporate entity.

Other judgments that will be analyzed concern those of international jurisprudence. In this way, the criminal liability of the business entity and its relationship with the purposes of the penalty in the context of the corporate entity will be studied in the following countries: United States, United Kingdom and Portugal.

BRAZILIAN JURISPRUDENTIAL EVOLUTION

The first analysis to be addressed on the subject of the functions of punishment in relation to the business entity concerns the national perspective. In this scenario, it is important to mention that several rulings will be analyzed demonstrating the change in the form of corporate conviction at the criminal level, both by the STF and the STJ, over the years.

The first judgment on the issue of liability of legal entities took place in the STF when deciding on the Ordinary Appeal in Habeas Corpus (RHC), number 66.102/SP on May 3, 1988, where Justice Moreira Alves was the rapporteur. On this occasion, which occurred shortly before the entry into force of the current Federal Constitution of 1988, the Supreme Court decided that there would be a criminal irresponsibility of the corporate entity, based on the societas non potest delinquere, because the analytical concept of the illicit was built based on the idea that human conduct governed and directed by the will would be necessary for the crime to be committed (Supreme Federal Court, 1988).

It so happens that, even with the entry into force of the current Federal Constitution, in the judgment of Habeas Corpus (HC), on March 16, 2004, number 83.301/RS, the 1st Panel of the STF, a scenario in which Justice Cezar Peluso was the Rapporteur, manifested itself with the intention of conferring, in a similar way, the criminal irresponsibility of the business entity. In the meantime, it was mentioned that business entities could in no way commit infractions, demonstrating that, despite the new constitutional scenario, the ideology was maintained (Brazil, 2004).

In a second moment, by the filing of the Special Appeal - REsp 564.960/SC, on June 2, 2005, with Justice Gilson Dipp as rapporteur, the Supreme Court of Justice decided in a single way for the company's criminal hetero-responsibility, overcoming the understanding now settled in the STF. For this new current, there would be a link between corporate responsibility and the denunciation of individuals who committed the unlawful act, who necessarily acted in the interest of society or seeking benefits for it (Supreme Court of Justice, 2005).

At this time, the STJ sought an intermediate point between the decisions coming from the STF, which carried the paradigm sustained for decades, and the constitutional mandate that subjects the offender, even if they are corporations, to criminal and administrative sanctions. It is worth mentioning that in this new scenario it is called the theory of double imputation. In fact, according to Professor Shecaira, the system of double imputation is the name given to the method of attributing criminal responsibility to legal entities, concomitantly with that of the individuals involved in carrying out the act (Shecaira, 2003).

Notwithstanding, the overcoming of the understanding settled by the STJ, through the aforementioned judgment, including in view of the new provisions in the scope of the current FC, as well as the words of Federal Law 9.605/98, there was a new judgment by the 1st Panel of the STF, with Justice Cezar Peluso being the same Rapporteur, on June 21, 2005, deciding, in RHC 85.658/ES, for maintaining the criminal irresponsibility of the business entity (Supreme Federal Court, 2005).

It is worth mentioning that in this part of Brazilian history on the criminal liability of the legal entity, it can be seen that, although there was theoretical permission issued by the Constitution and sanctioned by the Environmental Crimes Law, by the Supreme Court, the objective was to maintain the peaceful jurisprudence, brought even before the promulgation of the current Constitution, aiming at the unfeasibility of the criminal conviction of the collective entity.

In this context, it is not possible to draw a correlation between the three aforementioned judgments of the Supreme Court with the functions of punishment in relation to corporations, since it was decided that the latter was criminally irresponsible. Therefore, since there was no criminal penalization of the company until mid-2005 in the STF, there would be no room to deal with which theories would support the aforementioned purposes.

Also in 2005, by the analysis of HC 83.554/PR on August 16, 2005, with Justice Gilmar Mendes as Rapporteur, there was a decision for the hetero-responsibility of the legal entity in the criminal sphere. Thus, from this date, the understanding that was divergent among the higher courts, passed, by the aforementioned decision, for a pacification. Thus, in order for a certain company to be judged, it would be necessary to file a joint complaint with the individual who sought to bring advantages or benefits to it, according to the theory of double imputation (Supremo Tribunal Federal, 2005, p. 368-383.).

Therefore, from the second half of 2005, headed by the analysis of the Supreme Court of Justice, reaching the Supreme Court, there was a decision to overcome the societas delinquere non potest, taking into account the new provisions of the criminal legislation that brought scientific advances, new reasons, policies and criminal dogmatics, affirming the existence of the hetero-responsibility of the business entity in the criminal sphere.

With the existence of the possibility of criminal imputation to a business entity, the possibility of working on the functions of punishment is born. Therefore, if the criteria required by the theory of double imputation are met, applying the convictions allowed by law would be fulfilled in a practical way, considering the legal basis, the functions of punishment.

It is worth mentioning that, in this scenario, all penalties for business entities, even in the face of a typical, illicit and culpable fact, were conditioned to one more requirement, which is to investigate the transgression, before there is a criminal proceeding, to verify that the infraction was committed by a legal or contractual representative or also by a decision of the society's collegiate, to ascertain whether the illegality was committed in the interest or benefit of the entity, and, finally, to identify which individuals were involved in the situation so that there could be a joint complaint, as well as the conviction. Consequently, the functions of punishment were impaired in the same way, since in order to bring the retributive and preventive purposes to the crimes committed by the PJs, it would have as a sine qua non condition all the aforementioned extrajudicial stages.

Consolidating the theory of double imputation, the 1st Panel of the STF, on August 18, 2008, in the judgment of HC 92.921-4/BA, with Justice Ricardo Lewandowski as Rapporteur, despite the decision dealing with the impossibility of the business entity to file habeas corpus given the lack of reflection on ambulatory freedom, there was the reinforcement that, in order for the company to be condemned, there must be simultaneous denunciation with the individual who sought advantages or benefits for it, according to the theory of double imputation (Supreme Federal Court, 2008, p. 167-185).

Despite the limitation addressed by the 1st Panel of the STF, it is in this context of Brazilian history that the functions of punishment emerge. These functions, explored in detail in Chapter 2 of this dissertation, gain relevance when considering the need to hold both the business entity and the individual involved accountable, highlighting the punitive and preventive role of punishment within the scope of the theory of double imputation.

It should be noted that, as it was a change of understanding by the highest courts, such decisions impact all courts and lower courts, such as Federal Judge Barbosa, who stated in 2012 that without any doubt double imputation was necessary for the collective entity to be able to respond in the criminal sphere. Thus, the aforementioned judge mentioned that: "from the above, I conclude that it is not possible to penalize only the business entity in environmental crimes, in the wake of the prevailing jurisprudence currently in the distinguished TRF-1st region" (Barbosa, 2012, p. 270).

Likewise, Federal Judge Mário César Ribeiro also adheres to the thesis of the need for double imputation when he provided, and the other judges agreed, making the decision unanimous, that the criminal liability of collective entities in cases involving environmental violations is only accepted when there is simultaneous imputation of both the moral entity and the individual acting on its behalf or benefit (TRF-1st, 4th Panel, 2012).

Therefore, in this mentioned period of Brazilian history, there was a second moment of pacification of decisions, generating legal certainty, despite mitigating the functions of the penalty, since, for the application in a concrete case, as previously stated, prior investigations were required to determine the individuals involved in the crime.

Despite the aforementioned jurisprudential consolidation, this was short-lived, because in 2013, through an innovative decision rendered by the Federal Supreme Court, in the judgment of Extraordinary Appeal 548.181/PR on August 6, 2013, under the rapporteurship of Justice Rosa Weber, the autonomous criminal liability of the moral entity was recognized, thus giving rise to a scenario of corporate self-responsibility, without any need for concomitant imputation to the individual (Supreme Federal Court, 2013).

It should be noted that this position was considered an improvement of an isolated decision determined by the STF, in response to the AgRg in RE 628.582/RS, at which time the 1st Panel of that court, with Justice Dias Toffoli as rapporteur, on September 6, 2011, understood that although double imputation is necessary, double conviction would not be mandatory. Therefore, even if there is a need for a joint complaint with the individual, he could be acquitted without there being a negative repercussion for the purposes of a conviction against the business entity (Supreme Federal Court, 2011).

Based on this, the aforementioned Extraordinary Appeal 548.181/PR completely eliminated the need for double imputation, thus dispensing with the concrete identification of the individual who committed the offense on behalf of the legal entity and simultaneous imputation (Supremo Tribunal Federal, 2013).

It should be said that the vote of Justice Rosa Weber was very much supported by the studies of Professor Paulo César Busato and Professor Fábio André Guaragni, according to the former, there would be the nomenclature self-responsibility of the moral entity because there would be a new way of imputing a certain crime to him in a totally independent way of the figure of the individual. According to the professor, this model of responsibility, through analysis of criminal policies, criminological reasons and legal-criminal dogmatics, there was the perception that corporate transgressions had a hierarchical chain of command and pulverization of functions, which makes it challenging to identify specific individuals as perpetrators of certain violations. Finally, the Doctor brought the understanding that this new proposed model would not prevent any competition between the business entity and the individual who was in charge of the infraction (Busato, 2019, p.88).

About Professor Fábio André Guaragni, he, similarly to Professor Busato, states that the responsibility of collective entities does not eliminate that of the subjects who have been authors, co-authors or participants in the same act. The Doctor warns that the accountability of moral entities does not exclude that of natural persons, the objective is because the possibility of the company being condemned autonomously, in the criminal sphere (Guaragni, 2012, p. 136-137).

In this sense, it is noted that the paradigm shift that occurred in the Supreme Court was not aimed at the impossibility of criminal prosecution of the individuals involved, but at facilitating lawsuits against corporations, which are more easily identified in order to initiate a criminal process.

Still with regard to the aforementioned judgment, it should be clarified that, according to the vote of Justice Rosa Weber, it is not always appropriate to attribute a specific act to a single individual, since in certain situations the actions of a collective entity can be attributed to a group of individuals. The Minister also stated that the difficulty in identifying the person responsible leads to the impossibility of applying sanctions and that it is not mandatory to demonstrate co-authorship by the individual. It was demonstrated by the Minister that the decision to link corporate liability to individual liability would hinder the criminal prosecution of the former (Supreme Federal Court, 2013).

After a new understanding by the STF, the STJ modified its jurisprudence to adapt to the judgment of Extraordinary Appeal 548.181/PR, thus failing to apply the theory of double imputation to environmental crimes committed by companies. This fact occurred in the judgment of the Appeal in Writ of Mandamus No. 39.173 - BA, by the Fifth Panel of the Supreme Court, with Justice Reynaldo Soares da Fonseca as rapporteur, on 08/13/2015, a situation in which there was a judgment to maintain the criminal action against the Petrobras company, even after the acquittal of the natural person who committed the infraction (Supreme Court of Justice, 2015, p. 13).

Thus, when it comes to the functions of punishment, which are strongly related to the criminal liability of the corporate entity, they have undergone significant changes over the years, starting with a scenario in which there was no application in view of the criminal irresponsibility of companies, then moved on to the context in which the theory of double imputation was used, conditioned to the use of the functions of the penalty by the joint denunciation with the individual who was in charge of the criminal conduct, finally, due to the current circumstances, there is, by the criminal self-responsibility of the business entity, a direct application of the purposes of the sanction, being able to promptly impose the preventive and retributive character.

It should be made clear that the abandonment of the theory of double imputation does not exempt in any way the individuals who committed the criminal practice, being authors, co-authors or participants in the fact, as stated in article 173, paragraph 5, of the Federal Constitution and article 3, sole paragraph, of the Environmental Crimes Law, which say, respectively, that there will be a condemnation of the company "without prejudice to the individual responsibility of the directors of the business entity" and that of the "persons does not exclude that of natural persons, authors, co-authors or participants in the same fact" (Federal Constitution, 1988, p. 112; Brazil, 1998, p. 1).

Therefore, with the current way of holding the company responsible in a way that is disassociated from the individuals who committed the criminal practices, there is consequently room for the direct application of the functions of the penalty, so that, if there is proof of typical, illicit and culpable conduct, there will be the consequent application of the punishment tainted with the purposes of the punishment, in the manner provided for by ordinary legislators.

Thus, still dealing with the functions of the sanction, it is crucial to recognize that the application of the penalty to business entities should not be seen in isolation, but rather as part of a broader legal system. The approach to this topic requires not only a pre-application analysis, but also an in-depth understanding of the suitability of each purpose for companies, also verifying the practical application of prevention and retribution. Only then will it be possible to establish effective policies and procedures that promote fairness and integrity in the corporate sphere.

Finally, it is reinforced that this topic has relevance in terms of the pre-application of penalties, which, therefore, impacts the analysis of the functions of the penalty. With the self-responsibility of the enterprises, there is no longer the initial obstacle of double imputation, bringing even more relevance to the present dissertation. By suppressing such a barrier, the punishment of a given society is no longer conditioned to the identification of the culpability of an individual, which, in turn, enhances the viability of convictions, making use of the functions of the penalty.

International Perspective

The international perspective on the functions of punishment in the criminal liability of legal entities reflects a complex debate that involves an analysis of legislation, jurisprudence and some doctrinal opinions of the countries involved. At the outset, it should be said that each State selected for this work has a unique way of approaching the issue of criminal liability of societies. However, if there is punishment, there will be, linked to it, a common point of discussion, which is the purpose of punishment. While some legal systems emphasize punishment as a form of retribution, others focus on preventing future infractions. In addition, it is worth mentioning that the decisions of the higher courts play a crucial role in the interpretation and application of legal provisions, having a practical influence on the purpose of the sanction.

It should also be mentioned that the international analysis will take place in a qualitative way, seeking, in few countries, to analyze the purposes of punishment, both at the theoretical and practical levels. Thus, it will be possible to provide significant data on each selected country, contributing to scientific advancement. In fact, in view of the characteristics of the present work, it would not achieve the purpose for which the appreciation of many countries is intended, since it is necessary to study the entire legislative scenario, the related precedents and the related doctrine, as exposed below.

Therefore, the following countries were chosen to compose the study block of this chapter: United States, United Kingdom and Portugal.

United States

At the outset, it is worth saying that many points support the choice to analyze the United States-US scenario on this topic. The U.S. is recognized for its robust and highly developed economy, concentrating the largest global corporations. In addition, the extensive case law available makes it easier to understand legal practices and legal interpretations. It is also worth mentioning that the US has great global influence in legal and economic issues, making its criminal practices relevant and can be used as a reference in other countries. Such reasons justify the choice of the country.

The United States has, at the level of the legal system, a distinctive aspect of Brazil, which is the rigorous application of legal precedents. Thus, previous court decisions set standards for similar cases in the future, creating binding decisions that must be considered in future proceedings. In fact, both the Brazilian and the American legal systems have a Constitution, guaranteeing fundamental rights and guiding the creation and interpretation of laws in the country.

It is worth mentioning the jurist Ubiratan Junior, about the aforementioned system of precedents in the USA, when he asserts that: "The legal system of the United States is based on the principle of common law, which involves the application of judicial precedents to make decisions in similar cases in the future. The tradition of following previous decisions helps to ensure consistency in legal interpretations over time. State and federal courts play a fundamental role in the formation of common law, contributing to the evolution of legal rules and standards of justice" (Castro Junior, 2023, p. 2).

It turns out that, in the American scenario, although there are no direct constitutional norms that specifically deal with the criminal liability of business entities, the issue is dealt with mainly by specific federal norms and by Supreme Court precedents, which define the types of criminal conduct that can result in conviction for corporations.

Regarding the aforementioned federal laws, we can mention, as an example, two American laws that regulate the aforementioned liability, the first of which is the Foreign Corrupt Practices Act (FCPA), which was enacted in 1977, which aims to sanction American companies or companies with activities in the US that practiced bribery conduct to foreign officials. The second is the Sherman Antitrust Act, enacted in 1890, which aims to combat monopolistic practices and promote fair competition in the market, prohibiting restrictions on trade and anticompetitive practices (United States, 1977; United States, 1890).

In addition to this indication of infractions that would be compatible with legal entities, the various U.S. precedents establish requirements for such corporate criminal liability, which are: that the crime be committed by agents related to the corporation; that the agent has acted due to his position in the company; and that the action has generated any benefit to the company. It should be mentioned that the institution's condemnation remains even though it has expressly warned the employees not to commit a certain infraction (United States V. Jorgensen, 1998, p. 550, 560; United States V. Potter, 2006, p. 25; United States V. Sun Diamond Growers, 1998, p. 961).

On this fact, it is worth mentioning the case United States v. Park, which took place in 1975 and asserted that, in a free translation, "the criminal liability of the business entity could be based on the conduct of its employees and agents, provided that these acts are within the scope of its powers and for the benefit of the corporation". Thus, it was ratified that, as long as it is in control of the operations of the corporation, it will be responsible for the actions of its agents (United States V. Park, 1975, p. 658).

In addition to federal legislation that regulates the criminal liability of legal entities, precedents of the American Supreme Court also help in the delimitation of crimes that can be imputed to corporations.

In this sense, the American Supreme Court, at the beginning of the twentieth century, generated a precedent that remains in force to this day on the scope of the offenses that can be imputed to institutions. On that occasion, it was defined that in fact there are crimes that, by their very nature, cannot be imputed to the legal personality, however, the vast majority of crimes provided for in US legislation do not present incompatibility, thus allowing their application. Therefore, in this class of compatible violations, the agents of the company, acting by virtue of their function and seeking benefits for it, there will be the consequent liability of the aforementioned entity (New York Central & Hudson River Railroad Co. V. United States, 1909, p. 481, 494-495).

It is also worth mentioning the courts' understanding of the word "person" or the expression "whoever" provided for in the legal provisions, which cover, unless there is a positive rule to the contrary, the various types of companies, as well as individuals (United States V. A & P Trucking Co, 1958, p. 121, 123; United States V. Polizzi, 1974, pp. 856, 907; United States V. Hougland Barge Line, Inc, 1974, pp. 1110, 1114).

Bringing up the subject of double imputation, which was once a reality in Brazil, as exposed by the American jurist Charles Doyle, in a free translation, in the USA, "with rare exceptions, the statutes that expose the criminal liability of a company, do not absolve the directors, employees or agents whose violations are responsible for the company's situation" (Doyle, 2013, p. 5)

In short, the concept of double imputation, which was once a reality in Brazil, in the USA, the criminal liability of corporations does not exempt the culpability of the individuals who contributed to corporate violations.

It is worth mentioning that the decision to criminally prosecute a company in the US is up to the Department of Justice. It happens that few cases end with a criminal trial, since in the vast majority of cases the outcome is with one of the two types of agreements that can be made between the government and a citizen or society accused of a transgression. The first is the Deferred Prosecution Agreements (DPA), while the second is the Non-Prosecution Agreements (NPA) (Wayte v. United States, 1985, p. 598, 607; United States V. Nixon, 1974, pp. 683, 693; United States V. Armstrong, 1996, p. 456, 464).

A practical example of these agreements drafted by the Department of Justice occurred in United States v. JPMorgan Chase & Co.in 2014, when the financial services company, JPMorgan Chase & Co., agreed to pay the highest fine in U.S. history, in the amount of $13 billion, for having practiced fraud and manipulation in the marketing of subprime mortgages, which are the high-risk mortgages granted to individuals with bad credit, since it provided misleading information about the value and risk of these assets, also contributing to the 2008 financial crisis in the U.S. (United States V. Jpmorgan Chase & Co, 2014).

In addition to the financial burden, which has the function of retribution for the damages caused, but also the deterrence of future infractions, given that the financial burden was substantial, the company was compelled to implement a robust compliance program, with the objective of preventing similar situations. Thus, it should be emphasized that the retributive and preventive aspect of punishment is present in the American scenario.

Regarding the aforementioned retribution, punishment is seen as a form of return, to the agent, of the harm caused, similar to the absolute theory of national law. In the case of business entities, the remuneration aims to ensure that companies do not profit from illegal activities and that they pay for the damage caused to society. It is worth mentioning that this function of the penalty, although not expressly affirmed, it is possible to extract its application from some legal grounds, from precedents.

Regarding the legal basis for retribution, it is worth mentioning the Eighth Amendment to the United States Constitution, which prohibits the application of severe fines, including cruel and unusual penalties, which provides a guarantee that the punishments generally imposed in the judicial system are both fair and proportional to the seriousness of the crime. In this sense, it has the security that penalties are adequate, equitable and justifiable within the limits of the law (U.S., 1789).

Another legal basis concerns the U.S. Sentencing Guidelines, which would be the U.S. Sentencing Guidelines, functioning as a guiding system for the sizing of sanctions. Chapter 1, Part B, of these guidelines highlights the need to reflect the culpability of the defendant and the seriousness of the offense when determining the sentence, which ensures that the punishment is neither excessive nor insufficient. In fact, Chapter 5 deals with the imposition of the sentence and allows for additional adjustments to ensure that the sentence is adequate and fair, in line with the principle of retribution (United States Sentencing Commission, 2023).

In addition, Section 3553(a) of Title 18 of the United States Code establishes factors that courts must consider when imposing criminal sentences, and it is specified that there is a need to reflect in the penalty three criteria for achieving the purpose of retribution, the first is on the analysis of the nature and circumstances of the offense, the second refers to the seriousness of the offense and, finally, that a fair punishment for the crime is provided, thus bringing parameters for retribution of punishment (U.S. Code, 2023).

The case of United States v. JPMorgan Chase & Co. this is not an isolated situation, given that there was also a settlement in the 2017 case involving United States v. Volkswagen AG, in which Volkswagen AG was ordered to pay more than $4.3 billion in fines and penalties due to software installed in diesel vehicles to manipulate emissions test results. In addition to the substantial amount, there was an obligation to adopt a compliance program. Therefore, in terms of penalties applied and punishment functions achieved, the two cases reached the same outcome (United States V. Volkswagen Ag, 2017).

It should be mentioned that the penalty of substantial financial burden emerges as the primary tool of retribution and deterrence in criminal cases against legal entities in the United States due to its effectiveness in causing significant financial impact on companies.

Thus, the penalty of a substantial fine is a sanction that, as defined by the USA, serves several purposes, such as retribution and deterrence, both mentioned in the two judgments above. Even when associated with rehabilitation measures, such as the implementation of a compliance program, another purpose of punishment in corporate violations is achieved, which is the purpose of rehabilitating the offender.

Regarding the aforementioned deterrence, this is another function of punishment that has the purpose of discouraging potential offenders from engaging in illicit activities, through the imposition of penalties that are significant.

The deterrence is legally supported by Section 3553(a) of Title 18 of the U.S. Code, which directs courts on the need for sentencing to promote respect for the law, act as a deterrent to wrongdoing for the defendant and others, and protect the public from the defendant's future crimes. Thus, there is an imposition that sentences must deter future unlawful conduct, discouraging the defendant and all other members of society from committing crimes (U.S. Code, 2023).

After dealing with the purposes of retribution and deterrence, it is worth mentioning the studies of law professor Brandon Garrett on the increases in financial sanctions imposed on companies. In this sense, the professor alleges that in 2009, the highest criminal financial burden was 1.19 billion dollars, against Pfizer Inc., it turns out that in this same case, another billion dollars were paid to the government for the outcome of the civil action corresponding to the same fact. In fact, when he finished the case study, the aforementioned professor stated that the record substantial fine at that time was from a French bank, BNP, which made an agreement to pay the charge of 8.9 billion dollars, it turns out that this penalty was divided into a criminal fine of 4 billion dollars and a civil fine of almost US$ 5 billion paid to various regulators (U.S. Department Of Justice, 2015).

In this sense, there is a disproportionality between the civil financial burden and the substantial fine in the criminal sphere, considering that the latter should be the most onerous, but ends up being the opposite. This imbalance can weaken the impact of criminal penalty, by reducing its retributive and deterrent role, since civil financial burdens end up playing a more significant role than the punishment imposed by the penal system.

It should be noted that the Wall Street Journal studied the aforementioned BNP case, and analyzed that even with a conviction to a record sanction of 8.9 billion dollars, it was discovered that, for each dollar of alleged gains received, the bank paid only 0.27 to 0.30 dollars in fines, which demonstrates a disproportion between the profit resulting from the illicit act and the resulting punishment (Wall Street Journal, 2014).

Another example cited by Professor Brandon Garrett involves Standard Chartered, an international bank that pleaded guilty in the United States to violating Iranian sanctions, hiding about $240 billion in illegal transactions that earned it $7 billion in earnings. However, the bank paid only $674 million in combined civil and criminal fines (Garrett, 2016, p. 33, 40).

In addition to the aforementioned disproportions, Professor Brandon Garrett clarifies that, in a high percentage of agreements, there may not be any criminal sanction. The calculations made by the professor reflect that, between 2001 and 2012, of a total of 255 criminal cases against legal entities, 47% were finalized without the application of a criminal financial charge (Garrett, 2016, p. 33, 40).

It is worth mentioning that the examples brought above, according to Professor Brandon Garrett, are not considered exceptions, since he calculated that, between 2001 and 2012, the fines imposed on public companies represented, on average, only 0.04% of the total market value of these institutions (Garrett, 2016, p. 63).

When addressing the issue of corporate recidivism, which includes both the deterrent and rehabilitation functions, it can be stated that the occurrence of a subsequent crime by the same company indicates a failure in the application of one or both functions.

In this sense, in a study on recidivism only on financial institutions from 2001 to 2015 carried out by law professors Dorothy S. Lund and Natasha Sarin, they include: American International Group - AIG with enforcement proceedings in 2004 and 2006; Barclays Bank in 2010, 2012 and 2015; Credit Suisse in 2009 and 2014; HSBC Holdings in 2001 and 2012; J.P. Morgan three times in 2011, 2014 and 2015; Lloyds Bank in 2009 and 2014; Royal Bank of Scotland being convicted twice in 2013 and once in 2015; UBS Group was the one that committed the most recidivism and occurred in 2009, 2011, 2012,

2013 and 2015; and Wachovia which became Wells Fargo with executions in 2010 and 2011 (Garrett, 2016, p. 42).

A more current example that can be cited concerns HSBC, which reached an agreement in 2012 admitting to laundering money from drug cartels, being fined 1.9 billion dollars. It turns out that the following year, the same bank entered into another settlement for currency fraud, paying 110 million dollars. Finally, in 2019, the bank also entered into a third agreement to help customers evade taxes, paying the amount of US$ 192 million (Elstein, 2019).

Regarding this lack of deterrence and rehabilitation, preventing future crimes from occurring, Professor Brandon Garrett clarified that, despite being repeat offenders, they do not receive harsher penalties, even in the face of a growing criminal record (Garrett, 2016, p. 125).

What demonstrates with all the above is that the fines imposed on small and medium-sized companies have a substantial impact, effectively acting as a deterrent. However, when these sanctions are applied to large organizations, their proportionality decreases significantly, considering that despite reflecting large amounts, such amounts compared to the size of the corporation do not represent a true inhibition, which compromises the deterrent effectiveness of the penalties.

That said, it is possible to conclude that the North American system of application of substantial charges probably does not take into account the financial capacity of large companies as effectively when establishing penalties, which evidences a possible failure in the application of the functions of punishment, with a focus on the deterrence of illicit practices. It is true that, even if fines increase with criminal continuity, they are mild when measured as a percentage in a direct relationship with the assets or revenues of a large company in the market.

In the study carried out by law professors Dorothy S. Lund and Natasha Sarin, which gathered cases of recidivism by financial institutions between the years 2001 and 2018, it was observed that after the 2008 financial crisis in the USA, recidivism began to increase significantly. It is worth mentioning that of the crimes committed in 2010, only 7% dealt with recidivist companies, but in 2011 the percentage jumped to 28% and continued to increase until 2015 when it reached 50%, demonstrating that this year, with regard to financial infractions, half of the criminal executions deal with recidivist corporate entities (Lund, 2021, p. 338).

The conclusion generated by the aforementioned professors is that the substantial fines generate less-than-ideal deterrence, especially for the largest businesses, despite the constant record amounts. Demonstrating, according to the aforementioned professors, that, even in the face of very high sanctions, these are probably absorbed by the enterprise as a cost of doing business (Lund, 2021, p. 339).

In addition to the function of retribution and deterrence of crimes, the function of rehabilitation of the convicted organization was mentioned above, often associated with the implementation of the Compliance Program present in many criminal agreements. Regarding these agreements, it is worth mentioning that it is the responsibility of the Department of Justice not only to provide financial burdens to companies, with the use of substantial fines, but also, in view of the rehabilitation function, to impose structural reform practices, so that new internal controls, the demobilization of problematic businesses and the restructuring of products arise. Another common practice in criminal settlements concerns the hiring of an independent compliance monitor to oversee reforms.

Therefore, rehabilitation, which like the other functions is indirectly supported by Section 3553, is also one of the purposes of the penalty in the criminal liability of the USA. According to this section, it is the duty of the sentence to provide the defendant with training, education, medical care or other necessary corrections, which refers to the purpose of the convict's reintegration into society, seeking to minimize the probability of recidivism. Therefore, at first, the intention is to reverse the defendant's operational situation so that he can be reintegrated into the community (U.S. Code, 2023).

Likewise, rehabilitation is based on the U.S. Sentencing Guidelines, with some norms with a resocializing character, for example, in Section 5K1.1 it is allowed to reduce the sentence if the defendant provides substantial assistance to the government, in Section 6A1.2 it is said that the rehabilitation of the convicted person can be taken into account in the sentence (United States Sentencing Commission, 2023).

In addition, the issue of the rehabilitation of the business entity is also supported by precedents, as is the case of United States v. BP Products North America Inc., where an implementation agreement was concluded in 2007. In this case, there was an explosion at an oil refinery, where 15 individuals died and 170 were injured, BP agreed to pay a fine of approximately $50 million, and was required to implement extensive changes to its operations to prevent future incidents. Regarding the main measures adopted in the restructuring part of the company, it is possible to mention the extensive improvements in the safety and process management systems at the refinery, the emission control and reduction program, the hiring of external experts to conduct audits and implement recommendations, and committed to spending millions of dollars on safety and pollution control improvements (Rosenthal, 2009).

It so happens that the increase in recidivism mentioned above in the context of corporate crimes demonstrates a significant mismatch between the search for the company's reinsertion into society and the practical reality applied. Recidivism indicates that the companies, when they were again involved in illegal conduct, were not properly impacted by the rehabilitation measures, either due to ineffectiveness or lack of maintenance. Therefore, the penalties that should, theoretically, promote a structural change in society, preventing future infractions, end up having no practical support.

It turns out that the recurrence of corporate crimes does not demonstrate that compliance programs and other initiatives have no reason to exist, however, it clarifies that, the way the rehabilitations measures have been applied has not been able to inhibit the future practice of crime. Recidivism, therefore, shows that, in practice, the rehabilitation function of punishment is not achieving its purpose of transforming the offending business structures into legally responsible entities committed to ethics.

The fourth purpose of punishment under American law is incapacitation. This has similarities with neutralization in Brazilian law, because it aims to prevent future crimes by removing the offender's ability to commit new crimes. For individuals, incapacity usually involves deprivation of liberty, through prison sentences, in the case of business entities, incapacity takes a different form, such as the suspension of business activities.

A legislative example of this principle can be found in the application of the Sherman Antitrust Act, which is a federal law that combats monopolistic and anticompetitive practices. When a company is convicted of violating antitrust provisions, it may face severe penalties that include the dissolution of the entity, as a way to prevent the continuation of market-damaging business practices and promote fair competition (Sherman Antitrust Act, 1890).

Incapacity is affirmed in Section 3553(a) of Title 18 of the U.S. Code, guiding the courts on the need for the sentence to protect the public from the defendant's future crimes. Thus, it can be understood that neutralization is indeed a function of punishment in North American law (U.S. Code, 2023).

It so happens that, according to journalist John Markoff, in a study on the fate of the enterprises after the conviction, in which he analyzed the execution of companies between the year 2001 and 2010, he concluded that none of the defendant companies was put out of activity, demonstrating that under the terms of the agreement they avoid any possibility of these reputational costs (Markoff, 2013, p. 15).

Therefore, according to the analysis conducted by the aforementioned journalist, although there is a provision for a neutralization of the companies, this function of the penalty has no practical purpose (Markoff, 2013, p. 15).

Finally, it is only worth mentioning the restitution function, which aims to repair the damage caused to the victims, however, it has no practical application in the criminal area, acting only in the civil part of US law.

Thus, the functions of punishment in the criminal liability of business entities in the United States are: retribution, deterrence, rehabilitation and incapacitation, all of which are supported, even if implicitly, by the provisions of American legislation. Each of these functions has a crucial role in the justice system, having several practical means for them to be carried out. In addition, in summary, they have the objective of punishing, inhibiting future crimes, correcting corporate conducts protecting society and neutralizing the defendant preventing future transgressions.

However, in practice, for all the above, the application of these purposes has not proven to be efficient, even in the face of the imposition of considerable fines for large corporations. The execution of sentences often does not achieve the desired function, especially with regard to deterrence and the rehabilitation of offending companies. This disconnect between theory and practice compromises the ability of the punitive system to achieve its objectives, to ensure that the functions of punishment are effectively fulfilled in the criminal liability of business entities in the United States.

United Kingdom

Still from this perspective of international analysis on the subject, it is worth bringing to the examination the legislative and legal situation of the United Kingdom. Like the United States, the said nation represents one of the most advanced and influential economies in the world. In fact, the British legal system is known for its stability and the use of precedents, generating a solid basis for the investigation of judicial decisions. In addition, it is a country that carries much of the vision of Europe, although it is outside the European Union - EU, carrying comparative diversity for the present dissertation.

The UK legal system is based on the common law, which, like the US, is developed from precedents, making court decisions play a relevant role in the law. Furthermore, the United Kingdom does not have a codified constitution, but rather a collection of laws and conventions.

In the UK, the criminal liability of corporate institutions, at a theoretical level, is widely accepted and applied to a variety of entities, including companies, charities and local authorities. This possibility brings the British scenario too close to the American one, which allows for a vast degree of condemnation.

In this regard, it is worth mentioning that the UK Legal Commission, which is a body that keeps the law under review and recommends reforms if necessary, mentioned that from the beginning of 2020 until September of the same year, there were more than 5,000 convictions of legal persons, representing about 0.6% of all convictions. However, the agency states that it is for regulatory infractions, such as violations of environmental or commercial regulations, which are often created with corporations in mind (Ministry Of Justice, 2020).

It turns out that, although most criminal convictions against corporations are often associated with regulatory crimes, in the United Kingdom there is also accountability for serious offenses, such as manslaughter or fraud. In addition, a company can be complicit in crimes when they encourage or facilitate the commission of infractions by individuals.

However, despite the favorable scenario for conviction, it is worth mentioning that, from a practical point of view, the courts are guided by the main doctrine that governs the criminal liability of legal entities in this country, which is the doctrine of identification, also called the principle of identification. This principle establishes that, for an institution to be criminally convicted, the decision to commit the crime must come from the company's top management, such as the position of CEO, president, director and manager of the corporation. Therefore, if the "mental state" of the top executives is involved, there would be the possibility of judging the corporate entity.

In fact, as the author Regis Prado explains, the actions of the natural person, in high office, become the will of society itself. Therefore, according to the jurist, such individuals represent the will of the collective entity, and their will is the will of the corporation (Prado, 2013).

In this sense, law professor Gerry Ferguson asserts, in a free translation, that: "The doctrine of identification holds companies responsible only for the fault of employees or senior corporate leaders (i.e., the leading minds), and not for the fault of all employees, as occurs under indirect liability". It should be added that the aforementioned indirect liability, in British law, applies to civil law, but is generally not applicable to criminal law (Ferguson, 2019).

The High Court of the United Kingdom has stated that such individuals typically include the board of directors, the managing director and, depending on the specific case, other senior officers of the company. It should be mentioned that it was also held by that court that individuals to whom the board of directors delegated management functions, with complete freedom to act independently of the instructions of the board of directors, would also be classified as a "mental state" of the company (Serious Fraud Office V Barclays, 2018).

In this way, only individuals who represent the guiding will of the business can generate criminal liability for society, which reduces the scope of criminal rules, considering that not all unlawful conducts practiced by the corporation are supported by individuals with representative authority in the business entity.

It is worth mentioning that this approach does not go unscathed from criticism for its inability to properly deal with large-scale corporate misconduct. This is because, when large companies, such as banks, are sued for economic transgressions, even when these crimes are committed by relatively senior managers for the benefit of the institution, it must be evaluated whether the individual really had a management position in the company. In addition, in small companies the opposite occurs, as decision-making is more concentrated on the owner, it generates a much greater possibility of accountability when compared to large corporations.

In this sense, Vanessa Reid, who is a specialist in criminal defense and regulatory law, mentions, about the principle of identification, in a free translation, that:

This test has long been criticized, as it effectively limits the criminal liability of companies to crimes committed directly by the highest-ranking executives. Especially in the wake of a series of failed court cases, many commentators have criticized the old doctrine of identification as unjust and unfit for purpose. Under the "guiding mind and will" test, legal proceedings against large multinational companies with complex management structures were almost prohibitively difficult, as most directors and senior managers of companies were often too far removed from criminal conduct carried out on behalf of or within the organization. Smaller companies with simpler structures were exposed to a higher risk of criminal liability because they were easier to sue under existing doctrine, while larger organizations were able to protect themselves behind complex corporate structures while avoiding liability (Reid, 2023, p. 3).

It is worth mentioning that the doctrine of identification was born from the 1971 decision of the House of Lords, in the case of Tesco v Nattrass. In this trial, Tesco's lawyers argued, based on a previous civil case, that the actions of an attendant and a manager of a small store could not represent the direct will of the corporation, for it to be responsible for the unlawful conduct. In the specific case, Tesco was accused of misleading advertising by advertising a discount on a product that was not available in the store at the advertised price. The House of Lords agreed with Tesco, ruling that the manager did not represent the mind of the venture, and therefore Tesco could not be held criminally liable for the act. Thus, the company was acquitted of the criminal process (Tesco V Nattrass, 1972, p. 127).

Seeking to disassociate itself from the difficulties related to the principle of identification, the British Parliament has introduced new criminal laws that attribute criminal liability to companies for failure to prevent the occurrence of certain crimes. In addition, the aforementioned introduction of specific legislation aims to prevent unlawful acts, bearing in mind the role of correcting the problems associated with the principle of identification.

In this sense, it is possible to take as a basis three new examples of infractions created by the British Parliament aiming at the criminal liability of the legal entity, excluding the principle of identification, namely: corporate homicide; failure to prevent bribery; and tax evasion.

The first offense to be analyzed is the crime of corporate homicide and corporate manslaughter, present in the Corporate Manslaughter and Corporate Homicide Act, of 2007. This offence states that a company can be held criminally liable for homicide when its activities result in a death, due to the breach of duties of care (Corporate Manslaughter And Corporate Homicide Act, 2007).

The main point of this law for the present work concerns the sanctions applicable to the business entity. In this way, a convicted corporation can have against it the application of up to 3 punishments provided for in legislation, which are: unlimited fines, publicity orders (obligation for the enterprise to publicize the conviction) and remediation orders (duty to take measures to prevent previous failures; Corporate Manslaughter And Corporate Homicide Act, 2007).

Regarding the crime of failure to prevent bribery, this is provided for in the Bribery Act, created in 2010. The Associated Acts hold a corporation liable when a representative of the corporation offers or receives bribes, unless the corporation can prove that it has taken all appropriate steps to prevent the conduct (Bribery Act, 2010).

Regarding the possible penalties in this law that criminalizes bribery, there is the application of unlimited fines and, in serious cases, the exclusion from public tenders. Thus, it has a point in common with corporate homicide legislation, which is the possibility of imposing unlimited financial penalty (Bribery Act, 2010).

Finally, it is worth mentioning the law that punishes the facilitation of tax evasion, the Criminal Finances Act, of 2017. From this legal provision, if a legal entity fails to prevent its employees or associates from facilitating tax evasion, the corporation will be criminally punished with sanctions that include unlimited fines and, potentially, exclusion from public contracts (Criminal Finances Act, 2017).

Regarding the application of unlimited financial charges, provided for in each of the aforementioned laws, it is worth adding that, in practice, it proves to be the main penalty to be applied, and is usually the only one provided for in a sentence, as stated by the associate professor of law at Northumbria University (Roper, 2016).

In fact, the Law Reform Commission states that, except in the case of manslaughter and offences under the Health and Safety at Work Act 1974, the only penalties that can be imposed on a company under criminal law are financial, which would be the applicable fines, compensations and legal surcharges. It is worth mentioning that it would be possible to dissolve a company, in a few cases provided for in legislation (Reform Of Offences Against The Person, 2015).

It should also be noted that the creation of these laws demonstrates a new approach by the United Kingdom in attributing criminal liability to companies, imposing severe financial punishments and removing the difficulties of applying the identification doctrine, which requires proving the guilt of senior management under penalty of not condemning the organization.

In this sense, it is worth mentioning the theory of double imputation, which maintains that, in order to hold a corporate entity criminally liable, it is necessary that the individual involved in the situation is also prosecuted.

In the United Kingdom, the approach is different, but with some similarities to the theory set out above. As explained, the doctrine of identification, predominant in the British legal system, establishes that in order to prosecute and condemn an institution, one must identify and demonstrate the guilt of a citizen who acts in a position of senior management in the company. It turns out that, with regard to criminal complaints, in the United Kingdom, it is not required that the citizen be prosecuted or convicted simultaneously with the corporation.

Therefore, in the United Kingdom, there is no mandatory need for a double imputation, although, when using the doctrine of identification, to prove the liability of the business entity, it must demonstrate the guilt of a businessman or high-ranking official in the institution that has committed the act.

To analyze the purposes of punishment in the context of the criminal liability of business companies in the United Kingdom, it is necessary to consider both the legislation and the jurisprudence that has developed around this issue. Although the body of criminal law was originally designed with a focus on individuals, as the United Kingdom Law Commission adduces, this country has adapted its approach to address the reality of corporate infractions, recognizing the need for adequate and effective sanctions for institutions (Law Commission, 2021, p. 16).

The UK Sentencing Code, in its Section 57, sets out the legal objectives of punishment for citizens, which include: the punishment of offenders; the reduction of crime, with a view to deterrence; the reform and rehabilitation of offenders; the protection of the public; and reparation for victims. Thus, in practical terms, it is possible to mention that the United Kingdom, regarding the functions of punishment in the criminal liability of the individual, adopted retribution, deterrence, rehabilitation, neutralization, and reparation (Sentencing Code, 2020).

Although these principles apply primarily to individuals, they also serve as a reference in the condemnation of companies, albeit indirectly and adapted to the particularities of business entities, especially in view of the forms of sanction allowed in British law.

At the outset, it is worth making considerations about the penalty of a fine. It is worth mentioning that in the way it was designed in Brazilian law, this, being extremely limited, can only achieve the purpose of retribution for the crime, I do not have enough potential to, by itself, bring aspects of crime deterrence.

It is also worth remembering the scenario in the United States, where the application of substantial fines to corporations causes not only retribution for the offense committed, but, because they are severe financial penalties, they also play a deterrent role, which, consequently, discourages the penalized company and other corporations from committing similar infractions.

In the United Kingdom, the possibility of applying unlimited financial burdens in the criminal sphere to legal entities significantly reinforces the purposes of punishment, similar to the North American scenario, especially those of retribution and deterrence. The flexibility to impose potentially high financial penalties allows the penalty to be adjusted according to the severity of the offense and the financial capacity of the corporation, ensuring that the retribution is proportionate to the harm caused. This is particularly relevant in cases of large corporations, where a limited fine could be seen as just an operating cost, with no real impact on the company's conduct.

In this regard, the UK Sentencing Board Guidelines establish a multi-stage process for the conviction of enterprises. The first point to establish the penalty concerns the evaluation of the seriousness of the transgression, being a point of retributive character. Then, the court determines the turnover or the financial equivalent of the organization, this is a vital parameter for the application of the deterrent purpose, as there is an examination of the corporation that is committing the offense, in order to determine what for it would be a penalty with inhibitive capacity. After the application of the case-specific aggravating and mitigating factors, determined by domestic legislation (Sentencing Code, 2020).

Therefore, in the United Kingdom, to determine the ideal penalty, the court must consider the aspects of the seriousness of the infraction committed, but also the size of the companies, in order to ensure a punishment that is proportional to the organization's resources. There should also be an assessment of the impact of the financial sanction on the business's ability to compensate victims, improve its legal practices and the effect on the local economy, thus giving rise to a concern of the court to compensate victims and rehabilitate the offender (Sentencing Code, 2020).

Still on the deterrent function of unlimited fines, it is worth mentioning that, faced with the possibility of an unrestricted penalty, companies can adopt a more cautious stance and invest significantly in compliance and corporate governance, to avoid the occurrence of crimes. The threat of an unlimited financial penalty acts as a strong incentive for corporations to act within legal limits, contributing to a safer and more ethical business environment.

Regarding the deterrent function of penalties, it is worth mentioning the case of R v. Cotswold Geotechnical Holdings Ltd, of 2011, being the first conviction under the aforementioned Corporate Homicide and Corporate Culpable Homicide Act. Cotswold Geotechnical Holdings Ltd, which was a small geotechnical venture, was convicted after the death of a 27-year-old geologist, who died in 2008 when a trench collapsed while he was carrying out an inspection. The institution was fined £385,000, a sum that represented a significant sum for an organization of this size, with fewer than ten employees. The amount was projected to be paid over ten years, due to the company's small financial capacity, but still, the amount and decision were clear in reinforcing the importance of compliance with safety standards (R. V. Cotswold Geotechnical Holdings Ltd, 2011).

Another relevant case for the purpose of demonstrating the deterrent function applied to undertakings in the United Kingdom is that of R v. Balfour Beatty Rail Infrastructure Services Ltd, which took place in 2006. Balfour Beatty, one of the UK's largest infrastructure institutions, was condemned after a rail accident in 2000 that killed four people and injured more than 70. The organization was found guilty of breaching safety regulations, leading to the imposition of a fine of £10 million, as well as other legal costs. The high value served as a warning to other institutions in the sector, clarifying that the charges applied by the UK courts were as prepared to punish and deter both small companies and large organizations, as was the case in question, by imposing a severe financial penalty, in the loss of four lives and 70 injuries (R. V. Balfour Beatty Rail Infrastructure Services Ltd, 2006).

Finally, it is also worth mentioning the case of R v. Transco PLC of 2005. In this situation, the corporate company Transco was fined £15 million after a gas leak, due to lack of proper maintenance, causing an explosion that killed four members of a family. This amount, through surveys, was considered one of the highest ever imposed in the United Kingdom, compared to the damage of origin practiced by the legal entity. It should be noted that this sanction served not only as a retribution proportional to the seriousness of the offense, but also as a powerful instrument of deterrence (R. V. Balfour Beatty Rail Infrastructure Services Ltd, 2006).

Thus, through the analysis of the aforementioned cases, with the application of unlimited fines in the United Kingdom, there is evidence of the effectiveness of the deterrent function and the purpose of retribution of financial penalties in the business context. The possibility of facing unrestricted financial sanctions serves as a powerful incentive for companies to adopt rigorous compliance and governance practices, reducing the risk of infractions and promoting a more ethical business environment. According to the cases brought to the analysis, there was the desired effect of curbing reckless behavior and ensuring compliance with safety standards, reinforcing the responsibility of corporations, regardless of their size.

Regarding the rehabilitation function, mentioned in the United Kingdom's Sentencing Code, being one of the purposes of sentencing in the context of sentences for individuals, it aims at the reintegration of the convicted person into society, promoting behavioral changes that prevent recidivism (Sentencing Code, 2020).

When this rehabilitation function is brought to legal entities, as previously explored, there could be the implementation of compliance practices and other corrective measures that seek to transform the corporate culture, preventing future infractions and promoting legal compliance.

It turns out that, in the British scenario, the application of the rehabilitation function through criminal sentences to corporations is not common. Legislation and judicial practice have traditionally focused on functions such as remuneration and deterrence, with less emphasis on measures aimed at the rehabilitation of companies. In many cases, the punishments imposed on corporate entities focus only on the function of retribution and deterrence through fines and other financial sanctions, not focusing on the purpose of a rehabilitation, as would occur with the mandatory implementation of compliance programs.

Although there is a legal provision in the Corporate Manslaughter and Corporate Homicide Act that it is possible to order publicity and remedial order, which would play a role in promoting transparency and correcting specific flaws, they end up being, in fact, scarce, in practice, since the courts focus mainly on the penalty of unlimited fines, it is often the only one provided for in a sentence, as stated by the associate professor of law at Northumbria University (Corporate Manslaughter and Corporate Homicide Act, 2007; Roper, 2016).

It is noteworthy that the Legislative Reform Commission asserts that, with the exception of the case of manslaughter and offences set out in the Health and Safety at Work Act 1974, the only punishments that can be imposed on a corporate entity in criminal law are financial in nature (Ministry Of Justice, 2020).

Therefore, due to the total absence of provisions in sentences, the corrections proposed by the Corporate Manslaughter and Corporate Homicide Act are not sufficient or even the lack of standards that require the implementation of compliance programs, ethical training and measures to ensure that society behaves in a legal and socially responsible manner, with regard to rehabilitation standards, Failures in corporate ethics or management may persist, preventing a true transformation and a posture of resocialization.

It is worth mentioning the difference between deterrence and rehabilitation to understand how companies react to criminal sanctions. Deterrence focuses on discouraging illicit behavior through the imposition of severe punishments, seeking to inhibit the institution from committing crimes due to the cost and negative consequences. On the other hand, rehabilitation aims to promote an internal change in the culture and values of the enterprise, encouraging compliance not only out of fear of penalties, but through a conscious choice to act ethically and correctly. Even in scenarios where the fine imposed is relatively small, rehabilitation seeks to make the company take lawful and responsible practices, emphasizing integrity and commitment to legal and ethical standards, rather than just assessing the cost-benefit of illegal actions.

In this sense, although the application of the deterrence function to business entities seems to be enough to correct future criminal situations of corporate liability, it only inhibits a culture of illegal corporate practices, not generating a complete change in business values, where society, even in the face of a cost-benefit in practicing illegal conduct, would choose to follow the law, as would occur with the application of norms of a resocializing nature.

Therefore, although the rehabilitation function is central to individuals, in British law, there is not the same symmetry for companies, generating possible ethical challenges in the corporate context.

Another function of the penalty addressed by the UK Sentencing Code for citizens is to protect the public, so an analysis must be made to see its compatibility with business entities and how British courts behave towards this purpose. This protection of the public seeks to ensure that individuals who pose a risk to society are prevented from causing further harm, through measures that include restricting their freedom or imposing specific conditions (Sentencing Code, 2020).

As seen before in the analysis of the Brazilian and American scenario, regarding the compatibility of the application of the aforementioned function of protecting the public to institutions, it is possible to say that, even operating differently from individuals, it is a principle that can be applied to societies. This is due to the fact that, to the extent that certain criminal sanctions, such as the restriction of business rights or the temporary closure of business units, can neutralize the potential for a company to continue to cause harm to society, generating the purpose of corporate neutralization.

It turns out that, in the United Kingdom, the application of the function of protecting the public through criminal sentences to business entities, particularly in the form of neutralization of the company, such as restriction of rights or closure of units, is not a common practice. The emphasis of punishments for organizations focuses on financial aspects, as mentioned earlier.

An exception to the limited practice of neutralizing companies in the UK can be seen in the Bribery Act, which provides for the exclusion of corporations involved in such unlawful practices from future public tenders. This measure, while not resulting in a total closure of the business, could have a significant impact, especially for those that rely on public contracts for their operations. However, this form of neutralization is not enough for most companies, which can continue to operate in other markets and sectors. It turns out that the exclusion from public tenders can be understood more as a financial and reputational penalty than an effective neutralization, as it would limit the impact to a specific part of the business operations and leave other areas free for other activities (Bribery Act, 2010).

Thus, from what has been demonstrated, the British legal and legislative system tends to avoid sanctions that may lead to the stoppage of business activities, preferring other forms of penalty that seek to correct corporate behavior without compromising its ability to operate.

Finally, there is the function of reparation, present in the Sentencing Code of the United Kingdom, it is a purpose of the penalty intended to ensure that the offender compensates the victims for the damage caused. When considering the application of this function to corporations, redress can take the form of financial compensation or specific measures that seek to remedy the negative impact of corporate wrongdoing (Sentencing Code, 2020).

It is worth mentioning that there is compatibility of the reparation function with legal entities, given that the British legal system focuses, as stated by the Legislative Reform Commission, on financial penalties, which would be the applicable fines, compensations and legal surcharges. Therefore, courts can impose sanctions that not only punish but also correct the harm caused to affected parties (Ministry of Justice, 2020).

Thus, the case involving the company Sellafield Ltd, one of the largest nuclear energy institutions in the United Kingdom, ended with a conviction for improper disposal of radioactive waste, in violation of environmental and safety standards. The court imposed a financial burden of £700,000 and ordered the company to bear the costs of remediating the environmental damage caused. This demonstrates the concern with reparation, not only with the harmed citizens, but also with nature (BBC News, 2013).

Another case concerns Thames Water Utilities Ltd, a major developer in the water supply and sewage treatment sector in the United Kingdom, which was fined £20 million for allowing large amounts of sewage to be discharged into rivers and streams, causing significant environmental damage. In addition to the financial sanction, the company was required to carry out extensive cleanup and remediation of the affected areas, restoring the local ecosystem (Environment Agency, 2017).

Therefore, the function of redress in the criminal context in the United Kingdom, as demonstrated above, is oriented towards the correction of environmental damage caused by corporate infractions, aiming at the restoration and mitigation of negative impacts on the environment. However, direct compensation to subjects affected by infractions, such as individuals whose rights have been violated, is not traditionally addressed in the criminal sphere. Instead, such reparations for individuals are dealt with in civil law, which deals with awarding specific compensation and compensation to victims.

That said, in the United Kingdom, the application of the functions of punishment in the context of business entities demonstrates a robust focus on the purposes of retribution and deterrence, reflecting a tendency to impose severe punishments that discourage illegal corporate practices and ensure punishment proportionate to the harm caused. Unlimited fines are a clear example of how these functions are effectively met, ensuring that the penalty is significant enough to impact the company's conduct and protect society.

However, the UK has not demonstrated the same effectiveness in neutralization and rehabilitation functions in relation to organizations. Neutralization, which could involve more severe operational restrictions or the temporary closure of units, is not commonly applied, given that, as has been exposed, punishments are more focused on financial aspects. Likewise, rehabilitation, which involves cultural changes and internal practices in the company, is rarely addressed judicially, being limited to small aspects without promoting a true ethical transformation. This reveals a gap in the application of these criminal functions for companies, where the emphasis is placed predominantly on financial and deterrent aspects.

Finally, the function of redress in UK criminal law is mainly directed at the correction of environmental damage caused by corporate infractions, evidenced by cases such as the aforementioned Thames Water, which in addition to the fine, had to carry out the remediation of the affected areas. However, this function does not extend widely to direct compensation of individual victims, which is generally dealt with under civil law. Thus, while environmental redress is well incorporated into sanctions, personal compensation of affected parties is not a priority in the British criminal context.

Thus, in the context of UK criminal law, the functions of punishment applicable to legal persons are: retribution, deterrence and reparation, in certain terms. Retribution and Deterrence are well evidenced through the application of substantial fines and strict guidelines, ensuring that penalties reflect the seriousness of the crime and encourage compliant corporate practices. The Reparation function manifests itself especially in the correction of environmental damage, as observed in several cases. In this way, such functions maintain an incisive penalization of the corporation in the United Kingdom, ensuring practical responsibility for the business entity.

Portugal

The last country to be analyzed is Portugal, which, unlike the United Kingdom, is a member of the European Union, which makes it adopt and implement EU regulations and directives, thus bringing a robust and dynamic legal system. In fact, this country has advanced legislation in terms of criminal liability of legal entities, including strict measures against economic and financial crimes and against corruption.

Among the three countries analyzed in the international scenario, the Portuguese legal system is the one that most resembles that of Brazil, because both are based on civil law.

In Portugal, the criminal liability of companies is provided for in the Penal Code. In fact, the adoption of this liability arose from the reform introduced in the Code in 2007, and established a list of specific offenses for which legal persons can be convicted (Penal Code of Portugal, 1995).

Thus, in article 11 of the Portuguese Penal Code, it was established that corporations, with the exception of the State and organizations governed by public law, are liable to be held criminally liable for infractions committed in their name or in their direct or indirect interest, provided that such violations are committed by individuals who occupy positions of leadership or who act under their authority by virtue of a violation of the duties of supervision or control (Penal Code of Portugal, 1995).

In fact, article 11, paragraph 2, of the Penal Code, specifies the exhaustive list of crimes for which companies can be held responsible, including crimes against people, property, cultural identity and individual integrity, life in society, the State, and sexual freedom and self-determination. Thus, the Portuguese legislator sought to adapt criminal law to the specific sentencing needs of collective entities. It is worth mentioning that the recognition that these entities can commit unlawful acts has become evident (Penal Code of Portugal, 1995).

In addition, the Portuguese Penal Code provides for a set of punishments that can be applied to companies when they are considered responsible for infractions. The penalties that are titled as main in the legislation are fines and dissolution, while accessory penalties include measures such as prohibition of activities, prohibition of entering into contracts, deprivation of subsidies, and closure of establishments. It is worth noting that the choice of punishment depends on the seriousness of the crime and the specific circumstances of the case (Penal Code of Portugal, 1995).

As André Lamas Leite, PhD in Law, asserts, the penalty of a fine is the most common sanction applied to legal entities in Portugal. In fact, according to article 90-B of the Penal Code, the amount of the charge is determined based on the system of fine days, which can vary from 10 to 360 days, and on the daily value of the sanction, this "corresponds to an amount between 100 and 10 000 (euros), which the court sets according to the economic and financial situation of the convicted person and his expenses with the workers" (Penal Code of Portugal, 1995; Leite, 2020, p. 219).

It so happens that, when the secondary precept of the offense provides only for the punishment of imprisonment, the one referring to financial charges is calculated based on the conversion of the prison sentence into days of fine. Each month of imprisonment corresponds to 10 days of fine, according to article 90-B, paragraph 2 of the Penal Code. This allows for an adaptation of the punishment of imprisonment to a sanction applicable to business entities, while maintaining the proportionality and adequacy of the penalty (Penal Code of Portugal, 1995).

The penalty of dissolution, in turn, is considered a measure of ultima ratio, applied only in cases in which the existence of the corporate entity would be incompatible with the legal order. According to article 90-F of the Penal Code, this punishment can be applied when the business entity is used for the repeated practice of crimes or when its activity aims exclusively at the practice of unlawful acts, which generates the definitive closure of the corporation (Penal Code of Portugal, 1995).

There are also accessory penalties, which can be applied in a sentence when the seriousness of the violation and the specific circumstances of the case justify the need to impose additional sanctions to the main punishment. Accessory penalties are provided for crimes committed by institutions that demonstrate conduct that goes beyond a simple violation of the law. It is also worth mentioning that, in order for the application of the accessory penalty, there must be the imposition of the main punishment, which cannot be isolated in a sentence.

These accessory penalties play a complementary role, bringing to the legal system additional possibilities to control and sanction the activities of business entities, using, for example: prohibition of the exercise of activity, a period that can vary from six months to five years; judicial injunction, which symbolizes the fulfillment of certain obligations or the adoption of specific measures to prevent future wrongdoing or correct irregularities; prohibition of entering into certain contracts, can last between one and five years; deprivation of the right to subsidies, subsidies or incentives, can vary between one and five years; closure of a specific establishment; and publicity of the conviction (Penal Code of Portugal, 1995).

Regarding the theory of double imputation, it is worth mentioning that, both in the jurisprudential sphere, much defended by the Court of Appeal of Évora de Portugal, and in the doctrinal sphere, as stated by the jurist Anna Salvina Valenzano, the legal person can be held liable regardless of the conviction or acquittal of the agents. In this sense, although it requires the connection of the criminal fact imputed to the legal entity to an agent of the company, it does not require the conviction of the agent for the corporation to be convicted (Court of Appeal of Évora, 2012).

In addition, according to the judgment of the Lisbon Court of Appeal, of 13/07/2023, case: 940/20.0T9FNC. L1-5, which addressed the condemnation of the corporation, it was mentioned that "the liability of the legal person implies or depends on the individual liability of the respective agents (only not excluding their liability) the cumulation of both responsibilities for the practice of the unlawful act will not be a legal requirement" (Lisbon Court of Appeal, 2023).

Therefore, the Portuguese doctrine and judicial decisions, as demonstrated, as well as in the scenario of the USA and the United Kingdom, allow the legal person to be convicted regardless of the criminal liability of the individuals, making it possible to file a complaint, even unrelated to the identification of the agent who committed the unlawful act.

Regarding the purposes of the sanction for corporations, in the context of Portuguese criminal law, it is worth mentioning that they are extremely similar to the Brazilian ones, which have established criteria based on theories that legitimize the application of punishment. These theories are divided into two large groups: the absolute or retribution theories and the relative or prevention theories. The former justify the application of punishment based on the crime already committed, emphasizing the need for fair and proportional retribution for the harm caused (Figueiredo Dias, 1998; Palma, 2016).

For the absolute theory, punishment serves as a form of compensation, restoring justice through the punishment of the agent, without considering the future effects of the sanction. On the other hand, the relative theories justify the application of the penalty based on its preventive effect. There is also general prevention, which seeks to dissuade the community in general from committing crimes, either by the threat of punishment (negative general prevention) or by strengthening confidence in legal norms (positive general prevention). Special prevention, on the other hand, focuses on the delinquent, aiming to prevent him from committing new infractions. This can be positive, promoting the social reintegration of the agent, or negative, through neutralization (Silva, 2008).

Analyzing the criminal legislation, which aims to define the functions of the penalty, it is possible to mention article 40, paragraph 1, of the CP, which determines that the application of punishments and security measures aims at the protection of legal assets and the reintegration of the agent into society. This indicates that the criminal legal system in Portugal seeks to protect collective and individual interests, as well as aims at the rehabilitation of the offender, demonstrating a retributive, preventive and socializing orientation (Martins, 2011).

In this sense, it is worth mentioning that, based on a legislative analysis on the subject, the application of the penalty aims to ensure that the values and rights essential to living in society are preserved, aiming to ensure that illicit behaviors are punished, not only to repay the harm caused, but also to deter future infractions or even neutralize the agent, and thus protect the community.

In addition, article 40, paragraph 1, also mentions the reintegrating function of the penalty, which aims at the reintegration of the offender into society. This objective demonstrates that the legislator does not see punishment only as a form of punishment, but also as an opportunity for the agent to recover and reintegrate into the community, and this focus is aligned with the theory of positive special prevention (Penal Code of Portugal, 1995).

Article 40(2) establishes an essential limit to the application of the penalty: under no circumstances can the punishment exceed the measure of guilt. This principle of proportionality is a crucial element, ensuring that the penalty is fair and appropriate to the seriousness of the offense and the responsibility of the agent. It even reflects a concern with human dignity and with the limitation of the punitive power of the State, avoiding excesses and arbitrariness in the application of punishment (Penal Code of Portugal, 1995).

With regard to the determination of the concrete measure of the fine for business entities, article 90-B, paragraph 4 of the CP, in line with the aforementioned article 47, paragraph 1, refers to article 71, paragraph 1, of the same code, which stipulates that the measure of punishment must be set according to guilt and the requirements of prevention. Therefore, the determination of the penalty considers both the seriousness of the act, in view of the guilt of the offender, and the need to prevent future crimes, applying to both individuals and legal entities (Penal Code of Portugal, 1995).

Thus, in Portuguese legislation, the function of punishment goes beyond simple retribution, which is linked to the factor of guilt of the criminal, but prevention also occupies a central place. The punishment must be sufficient to prevent new crimes, both on the part of the convicted person and by deterring other potential offenders. This evidences the adoption of a mixed view, which combines retributive elements with a strong emphasis on prevention and rehabilitation.

About these facts, the jurist Ana Sofia Rodrigues Pereira states that "by limiting the preventive end of punishment with the judgment of guilt, the legislator enshrines a preventive-ethical conception of punishment and avoids the criticisms of disregard of the individual that are usually pointed out to purely utilitarian theories of prevention". In fact, the aforementioned jurist adds, that when the legislation mentions preventive functions, it is linked to both the general and the special functions (Pereira, 2018, p. 53).

It so happens that, due to the existing limitation of the criminal sanction to the guilt of the agent, as the jurist Ana Pereira also clarifies, the preventive requirements of punishment cannot, under any circumstances, be imposed at an extreme level. This is due to the fact that the agent, in the way in which Portuguese criminal law was constructed, the agent cannot be used as an example for the rest of the community (Pereira, 2018, p. 58).

In Portugal, regarding the various judicial decisions, it is worth mentioning the case no. 82/20.9GEACB-A. C1, decided by the Court of Appeal of Coimbra, on February 2, 2022, involving a company convicted of violating safety standards, which resulted in the death of a person. On that occasion, the aforementioned court sentenced a daily fine of 300 Euros, for 480 days, which totaled 144,000 Euros (Court of Appeal of Coimbra, 2022).

It is worth mentioning that the decision took into account the company's economic situation and labor charges to determine the daily rate of the sanction, considering the seriousness of the infraction. In this way, it reflects the function of retribution of punishment by establishing a daily fine of 300 euros, aiming to ensure that the penalty is proportional to the damage caused and the financial situation of the company, which reflects the intention of a fair and adequate criminal response, fulfilling the function of retribution. Therefore, judicial decisions reflect a concern to ensure that the sanction is proportional to the degree of culpability of the business entity, as well as to the impact of the crime on society.

Another example of the application of the function of retribution of the sentence occurred in the judgment of the Court of Appeal of Évora, delivered on 10 May 2016 (case no. 1966/13.6TAPTM. E1), the decision to dismiss the appeal established that the rule of Article 90-B(5) of the Criminal Code, which sets a minimum limit of 100 Euros for the daily amount of the fine penalty, is not unconstitutional. This rule is considered valid when applied to business entities who face serious economic difficulties in subsistence or who no longer operate and only have debts, in view of the culpability of the same in the specific case (Court of Appeal of Évora, 2016).

Finally, it is worth mentioning the judgment of the Court of Appeal of Coimbra, case no. 194/13.5IDLRA. C1, judged on 04/02/2015, where it was established that the daily amount of the fine, in addition to considering the culpability of the business entity, "must be fixed according to the economic and financial situation of the convicted person and his or her burdens" (Court of Appeal of Coimbra, 2015).

That said, the three cases exemplify how the Portuguese courts consider the function of retribution of the penalty in the criminal liability of corporations. In judgments, courts not only assess the economic capacity of companies, but also the seriousness of the infractions and the culpability involved.

It so happens that there is a criticism about the possibility of analyzing, at an academic level, this aforementioned assessment of the economic capacity of companies, in order to have an assertive application of the function of retribution of punishment in the criminal liability of business entities in Portugal. In this sense, it is worth mentioning that, in order to have a detailed approach to the subject, exempting the compatibility between what is sought in theory with the functions of punishment and practice, it is required to have the identification of the convicted corporations, which does not occur. Although the Portuguese legal system recognizes the importance of the retributive function in the criminal accountability of institutions, and mentions in judgments that this function is applied, it is not possible, at the international academic level, to study whether, in fact, it is being applied.

As demonstrated, based on remuneration, in the case of legal entities, fines, being the main sanctions, must reflect both the seriousness of the infraction and the economic capacity of the institution. However, the lack of transparency in the identification of the condemned company, as in case no. 82/20.9GEACB-A. C1, judged by the Court of Appeal of Coimbra, makes it totally impossible to study the economic capacity of the corporation, which is vital to assess whether the penalty really fulfills the retributive function (Court of Appeal of Coimbra, 2022).

It was observed, through a search on Google Scholar, Google Search and by each website of each court in Portugal, that in legal proceedings, there is the replacement of the names of the organizations by generic identifiers, such as "AA", which prevents an in-depth analysis of whether the penalty applied is adequate to the financial and operational reality of the company in question. Unlike the individual, where the identity of the convicted person is, in many cases, irrelevant to the analysis of the proportionality of the punishment, the case of imprisonment is cited, where, in most cases, the analysis of who is being sentenced does not depend to determine whether the punishment is fulfilling the retributive effect. In the case of companies, the financial context and the size of the corporation are crucial in determining whether the fine imposed actually fulfills the retributive function.

In addition, the omission in the identification of convicted companies makes it difficult to analyze recidivism and understand the effectiveness of penalties in preventing new crimes. Without access to the institution's identity, it is impossible to verify whether it has a history of infractions, which would be essential to assess the need for harsher punishments or stricter compliance measures.

The function of retribution cannot be dissociated from the inhibition of crimes, and the lack of transparency undermines the analysis of negative general prevention, which aims to threaten society through serious punishment, thus dissuading the practice of similar crimes. This is because, when applying penalties to unnamed companies, a study cannot be carried out to determine whether or not there is rigidity in the financial capacity of corporations.

In summary, the lack of transparency in the identification of companies convicted in Portugal undermines the practical application of the function of retribution of the sentence, as well as the general negative prevention. Although legislation and jurisprudence show a concern with the proportionality of penalties, without the possibility of identifying the organizations involved, the analysis of the adequacy of sanctions is severely compromised.

Regarding the general positive prevention in the context of the criminal liability of legal entities in Portugal, this concretizes the function of punishment of demonstrating the validity of the laws and confirming the values legally protected by society. However, when contrasting this principle with the available statistical data on the conviction of legal persons, we realize that the effectiveness of general positive prevention is somewhat limited, but possible. Acquisitive crimes, being those committed with the objective of obtaining goods or financial advantages, are the predominant among the infractions committed by corporations, as stated by law professor André Lamas Leite (Leite, 2020, p. 218-219).

According to the Directorate-General for Justice Policy of Portugal, in a study carried out between 2008 and 2018, about 1,600 transgressions involving companies and equivalent entities were recorded in Portugal in the last year of the survey. This acquisitive crime was the most common, followed by infractions against life in society. It should be mentioned that, from 2008 to 2013, crimes against property and patrimony, carried out by corporate entities, increased from around 200 to about 1,700, followed by a decline until 2016 and a slight increase until 2018 (Directorate-General for Justice Policy, 2018).

In conclusion, although general positive prevention aims to reaffirm the validity of laws and the values protected by society, effectiveness in practice has been limited. Statistical data show that, despite the intention to deter illicit practices through the application of sanctions, acquisitive crimes continue to be predominant among infractions committed by business entities. The significant increase in crimes against property and patrimony between 2008 and 2013, followed by fluctuations until 2018, suggests that the application of penalties, although existing, has not been fully effective in preventing these conducts.

This highlights the need for continued analysis and possibly enhancement of punitive measures to ensure that the positive general prevention function can fulfill its role more robustly in practical reality. This shows that the threat of penalties, although present, has not been sufficient to deter the commission of such crimes (Directorate-General for Justice Policy, 2018).

Regarding the special positive prevention in Portugal, which has the resocialization of offending corporations as a function of the penalty, avoiding recidivism and promoting the reintegration of these entities into society, it is worth mentioning that part of the Portuguese Penal Code, article 40, no. 1, which makes explicit reference to the reintegrating function of the penalty, showing that the Portuguese legislator does not see punishment only as a form of punishment, but also as an opportunity for the recovery and reintegration of the offender into the community (Penal Code of Portugal, 1995).

In the case of business entities, the penalties affirmed in Portuguese legislation, unlike US legislation, for example, because they are limited to the culpability of the agent, do not attribute a dissuasive sanction, nor do they seek the imposition of compliance and corporate governance, the only penalty that would be able to positively change the business scenario would be the publicity of the condemnatory decision, Considering that, this would cause a shake up in the image of society.

In addition to the publicity of the sentence, as measures that would have another main focus, but which also serve rehabilitation, the following can be mentioned: prohibition of the exercise of activity; judicial injunction; prohibition on entering into certain contracts; deprivation of the right to subsidies, subsidies or incentives; and closure of a specific establishment. It should be noted that although they seem to be sanctions with extreme harmful potential for companies, they will always be governed by the maxim of corporate culpability, not being governed by the deterrent effect.

Before entering into the practical aspect of rehabilitation, through the symmetry of penalties, it is possible to address beforehand the theory of special negative prevention in criminal law, which has as its main objective to prevent the convicted entity from committing new crimes again, ensuring this prevention through the neutralization of the offending agent. As seen before, in the case of legal entities, this incapacitation does not occur by deprivation of liberty, as occurs with individuals, but by the application of penalties that limit or prevent the continuity of illicit practices by the entity. Accessory punishments play a crucial role in this context, acting as mechanisms to control and restrict the company's activities to ensure that it does not commit crimes again.

The prohibition of the exercise of certain activities or the temporary closure of the establishment where the crime occurred, there is, in fact, a neutralization of the risk of recidivism. In addition, the prohibition of obtaining public subsidies or subsidies can also be seen as a form of special negative prevention, since it seeks to limit the conditions that could facilitate the commission of new crimes.

From a practical point of view, it is worth mentioning the judgment of the Lisbon Court of Appeal, case no. 1104/17.6Y5LSB. L1-5, Rapporteur Paulo Barreto, dealt with an appeal related to the autonomous liability of a legal person in the context of an administrative offence, an offence of an administrative, unlawful and sanctioned nature. It is worth mentioning that, although it is not exactly a crime in criminal law, a relevant fact of legal innovation was discussed, where the Portuguese court mentioned that "this autonomous liability is particularly important today, especially due to the so-called compliance programs, which, if effective, may lead to the irresponsibility of the legal person, as already provided for in article 31 bis of the Spanish Penal Code (in Italy and France there are regimes that approach)". This is mentioned by European legislation as friendly criminal law (Lisbon Court of Appeal, 2021).

Rehabilitation, in the context of business entities, is not limited to punishment or simple reparation of the damage caused, but involves the structural transformation of the company to avoid the repetition of unlawful conduct. The implementation of an effective Compliance program is essential to achieve this change, as it establishes internal control mechanisms, promotes an ethical organizational culture and ensures compliance with the law.

In this way, the adoption of Compliance programs not only contributes to the resocialization of enterprises, but can also act as a factor of mitigation or even exclusion of criminal liability, encouraging corporations to adopt more responsible business practices in line with legal and ethical principles.

Finally, it is worth mentioning the judgment of the Lisbon Court of Appeal, case no. 1874/19.7T8TVD. L1-5, which deals with an appeal for environmental offense where the appellant institution was convicted of carrying out expansion works on a property located in an area classified as a National Ecological Reserve, without obtaining the proper administrative license permit. The Court decided that, considering the seriousness of the infraction and the economic impact on the small company, it would be appropriate to suspend the execution of the fine, provided that there was an additional penalty that would be the restoration of the situation prior to the infraction (Lisbon Court of Appeal, 2021).

In this way, the neutralization of the legal entity is evidenced, by imposing that it not only stabilize the irregular construction, but also restore the place to its original state, directly reflecting the function of the special negative prevention of the penalty. This function aims to prevent the entity from relapsing into the practice of crimes, ensuring that the damage caused is completely reversed and that the corporation is discouraged from committing future infractions.

Therefore, special negative prevention is effective by ensuring that the legal entity not only stops the irregular conduct, but also reestablishes the previous conditions, reinforcing the idea that the penalty should protect society from future unlawful behavior.

Finally, with regard to the practical aspect, it should be mentioned that, according to the Directorate-General, with regard to punishments, fines were the most applied, representing about 4% of total convictions in 2013, while substitute penalties represented less than 0.5%. The dissolution of business entities was rarely applied, becoming statistically insignificant (Directorate-General for Justice Policy, 2018).

In conclusion, in the context of the criminal liability of legal entities in Portugal, a complex approach to the functions of punishment is observed. The Portuguese legislation, by providing for the application of penalties to corporations, reflects a clear retributive orientation, which aims to punish the agent according to his guilt, without the need to be linked to the criminal responsibility of individuals. In addition, the Portuguese legislation and doctrine, mentioned above, also incorporate preventive aspects, both general and special.

It so happens that, in practice, according to all the above, due to the lack of transparency in the appointment of the condemned companies, it was not possible to analyze a compatibility between what is sought by the legislation and what is reflected in the various Portuguese courts. In addition, therefore, the practical examination of general negative prevention, which seeks to dissuade society in general from committing crimes, through the threat of sanctions, cannot be analyzed with scientific rigor either, considering that, by ignoring the penalized companies, the punishments, especially the financial ones, can be extremely significant or insignificant, depending on the size of the corporation.

On the other hand, the general positive prevention, which aims to reaffirm the validity of legal norms and social values, the practice, according to statistical data, has been shown that its effectiveness is still limited, particularly in the case of acquisitive offenses, which continue to predominate among the infractions committed by legal entities, with large numbers and growing.

Regarding special prevention, in turn, it is divided into positive and negative. The positive one, although restricted to accessory penalties, aims at the resocialization of the institution, preventing recidivism and promoting the reintegration of the company into the market and society. However, the lack of sanctions that are targeted at strengthening corporate governance and regulatory compliance limits the potential of this function. Regarding the special negative prevention, this does have practical compatibility, having several penalties structured in law to neutralize the business entity, preventing the repetition of crimes, imposing restrictions that aim to protect society, it is only worth mentioning that, as seen before, it has little application by the Portuguese courts, with the penalty of a fine being the most frequent measure.

Finally, the lack of transparency in the identification of companies convicted in Portugal emerges as a significant obstacle to the academic analysis of this work, especially in relation to the function of retribution and deterrence, in the form of threats, of the penalty. Without this identification, the evaluation of the proportionality of punishments and the understanding of their effectiveness in preventing new crimes are compromised. In addition, the other functions provided for in Portuguese legislation, namely, confirmation of values, rehabilitation and neutralization, need legislative and legal adjustments to achieve full effectiveness. Thus, the practical implementation of the functions of punishment in the criminal liability of legal entities in Portugal still faces challenges, especially with regard to transparency and the adequacy of sanctions to the reality of the corporations involved.

CONCLUSION

The analysis of the functions of punishment in the criminal liability of legal entities reveals the complexity and diversity of approaches in different legal systems. Throughout this work, it was explored how the theories of retribution, respect for the law, deterrence, rehabilitation and neutralization are applied in different ways in countries such as Brazil, the United States, the United Kingdom and Portugal. Each country, in dealing with corporate infractions, seeks to balance the need to punish, prevent and, in some cases, rehabilitate business entities, reflecting their own legal and cultural traditions.

Initially, after examining the theories that qualify business entities in Brazilian law, the criminal liability of the corporation was explored, as well as associated limitations. In the meantime, it is worth mentioning that, in Brazil, the criminal liability of companies is limited and applies mainly in cases of environmental crimes, as established by the Federal Constitution and the Environmental Crimes Law. In fact, the condemnation of companies depends on acts committed by their legal representatives or collegiate bodies, acting in the interest or benefit of the entity. Thus, the criminal trial of business entities in the Brazilian scenario is restricted and specific (Brazil, 1998; Federal Constitution, 1988; Júnior, 2022, p. 13).

Making a parallel with chapter 3 of this dissertation, which deals with a comparative analysis between the legal scenario of Brazil and that of the United States, the United Kingdom and Portugal, it was realized that corporations can commit several criminal types, far beyond the branch of environmental law. In fact, in the United States and the United Kingdom, the rule is that all the crimes provided for can be committed by a legal entity, unless there is total incompatibility. Portugal, in turn, defines in legislation all the unlawful acts that can be committed by society.

It is worth considering, also in the international analysis, that, in the American case, the company can be penalized only for acts committed by its agents, within the scope of their functions and benefiting society. In the United Kingdom, there is the doctrine of identification, which limits the criminal liability of corporations to the actions of the company's senior managers, with few exceptions to this theory. Finally, regarding Portugal, there are corporate wrongdoings when committed by people in leadership positions or by their subordinates due to the failure of surveillance or control (Ferguson, 2019).

Before entering into the subject of the functions of punishment, it is worth mentioning the penalties being provided for in Brazilian legislation and comparative law, since these are the main limiting factors of the practical field of the purposes of sanction. Therefore, presentation at work has become essential.

Thus, in relation to penalties, Brazil provides for three main types of sanctions for business entities: fines, restriction of rights and provision of community service. These punishments are applied taking into account the seriousness of the offense and the benefit obtained by society. In the United States, the financial burden is always provided for as substantial, aiming at retribution and deterrence of crimes, and is even the most common penalty of application, according to local jurisprudence and doctrine. In addition to fines, companies may be required to implement compliance programs or even face dissolution in extreme cases, such as those provided for by the Sherman Antitrust Act (Brazil, 1940; Sherman Antitrust Act, 1890).

In the United Kingdom, penalties for business entities include fines, but they are more severe than in the American case, being already provided for without any maximum limitation, being the most frequent sanction, in addition to there are also punishments of exclusion from public contracts, remediation orders and advertising orders. Portugal, finally, also adopts the financial burden as the main punishment for business entities, in addition, it has accessory penalties, such as the prohibition of activities and the closure of establishments and, in more serious cases, the dissolution of the company.

It should be mentioned that, in the face of an exhaustive study on penalties, although the four countries share the use of fines as a penalty for business entities, the approaches are different. In Brazil, in view of the stricter sanctions, in relation to the maximum limit, fines, according to the doctrine, according to criminalist Marina Coelho Araújo, start to serve only the function of retribution of punishment, not having the capacity to generate preventive effects, in view of the financial ceiling that can be applied in the specific case (Coelho Araújo, 2017, p. 183).

On the other hand, the United States and the United Kingdom, respectively, provide for substantial and unlimited fines as sanctions to business entities, emphasizing not only retribution, but also deterrence, present in preventive theories of punishment. Portugal adopts a system similar to the Brazilian one, where both fines and other accessory penalties are limited to the culpability of the agent, that is, in no way can the punishment exceed the guilt of the agent, not even for deterrence purposes, limiting the financial burden to the retributive purpose.

Really entering into what is proposed in this research, which is the analysis of the functions of punishment in the criminal liability of the business entity, it is worth mentioning, at the outset, that they seek to justify criminal intervention in a logical and rational way, especially in the Brazilian scenario, through the purposes of retribution, treated by the absolute theory, and prevention, addressed by the relative theory. It should be mentioned that these functions are not limited to only one branch of law, which in this case is Criminal Law, but are linked to the forms of sanction treated individually.

Regarding the function of retribution of the penalty within the scope of the criminal liability of legal entities, it is worth mentioning that this purpose is based on the idea that the punishment should correspond to the harm caused, seeking only to sanction the unlawful conduct.

Regarding the aforementioned purpose of retribution of punishment, in Brazil, the Penal Code asserts that the sanction must be necessary and sufficient to disapprove the crime, reflecting the need to punish the agent for the offense committed. Thus, there must be proportionality between the penalty and the seriousness of the crime, which is a central principle (Brazil, 1940).

After extensive analysis, it became evident that, in the Brazilian scenario, the penalty of a fine is the one that best meets the purpose of retribution in the context of the criminal liability of business entities. This statement is based on the intrinsic nature of the fine, which imposes a direct financial cost on the offending company, functioning as a response proportional to the damage caused and, in addition, is based on the maximum legal limit that can be imposed. The other penalties, such as the limitation of rights and services to the community, have different objectives, guided mainly by prevention. They aim to prevent recidivism, through various inhibitory practices, such as neutralization and rehabilitation of the agent, thus functioning as prevention measures, having little retributive character (Coelho Araújo, 2017, p. 183).

Still on the Brazilian scenario, it is observed that, in practice, the fines applied are much lower than the actual damage caused to the environment by corporations, which raises questions about the effectiveness of retribution in punishing legal entities in Brazil, especially in cases of great impact.

The Samarco Case illustrates this discrepancy well. Despite the seriousness of the environmental damage caused by the dam collapse, the maximum fine that could be imposed on the mining company Samarco by the criminal sphere would be approximately R$127,656,000.00, which represents only 0.2684% of the estimated value of the total loss, which was R$47.6 billion. That amount is insufficient to adequately reflect the seriousness of the damage, limiting the effectiveness of the retributive function of the penalty. Therefore, it reveals a failure to achieve the true retribution that the absolute theory of punishment intends. In view of this example, and many others presented in the course of this research, the retributive function of punishment is not effective in Brazilian practice, resulting in unsatisfactory and insufficient retribution for serious environmental damage and other large-scale crimes (D'Agostino, 2015).

In the United States, retribution is equally central, but in view of the substantial fines provided for in the legislation, the application is in such a way as to ensure that societies do not profit from illegal activities and pay for the damage caused to society. In fact, the billionaire financial charges applied in cases of corporate fraud reflect the intention to punish companies proportionally to the damage caused. Retribution, therefore, is aligned with the idea of retributive justice, where punishment must reflect the harm caused and bring the agent damage proportional to his act.

There is, therefore, no practical incompatibility in the application of this function of punishment, since the legal and judicial structure of the United States is designed to ensure that sanctions are carried out effectively. It should be noted that the effectiveness of the application of retributive penalties is reinforced by the rigor in the execution of sentences.

In the context of the United Kingdom, the doctrine of retribution is also applied, aiming to punish the company in proportion to its liability for the unlawful acts committed. The application of fines in the UK is flexible, with the possibility of unlimited financial burdens in some cases, which reflects a strong emphasis on proportionate punishment. However, it should be mentioned that although there is effectiveness in achieving retribution in the application of penalties, the United Kingdom faces challenges in the condemnation of societies, especially in the context of the doctrine of identification, where corporate guilt emerges when committed by key individuals in society, which greatly limits the imposition of sanctions.

The function of retribution of punishment plays a central role in the criminal accountability of business entities in the Portuguese scenario, where sanctions are designed to reflect the seriousness of the infractions committed and the economic capacity of the convicted companies. Portuguese jurisprudence has consistently affirmed the importance of ensuring that penalties are proportionate to the damage caused and the financial situation of the corporations involved.

It so happens that the academic analysis of the practical effectiveness of this function is compromised by the lack of transparency in the identification of convicted companies, limiting the possibility of verifying whether the sentences really have the retributive purpose in their core, limiting the evaluation of the proportionality of the penalties and the effectiveness of the criminal response.

Another essential function of punishment, which is equally applied in all the countries studied, is general negative prevention, which focuses on deterring future illicit behavior, through the threat of having a penalty imposed against oneself in criminal law.

In Brazil, the application of the theory of negative general prevention, in the context of business entities, can be applied effectively in some aspects, in view of the possible sanctions at the level of disqualification, that is, penalties restricting rights, which generate sufficient threat to companies to inhibit the practice of crimes. In this sense, it is worth noting that this function of punishment seeks punishments considered severe, in order to discourage future equally illicit conduct, generating an example for others in society.

As seen before, due to the maximum limitation of fine penalties in criminal law, this would not bring the inhibiting aspect, however, the punishments restricting rights proved to be effective, as they provide for the "partial or total suspension of activities; temporary interdiction of establishment, work or activity; and prohibition of hiring, obtaining subsidies, subsidies or donations from the Government", which generate an effective shake-up in business activities, thus emerging as an inhibitor of the practice of crimes.

In the American context, the deterrent function of penalties against legal entities is widely accepted by the use of substantial fines, which are seen, in addition to retribution, as an effective form of deterrence, as they have the ability to financially impact companies, forcing them to reconsider their practices and policies.

It is only necessary to point out that, scholars, as previously pointed out, indicate that, despite the high amounts involved, the real impact of fines can be minimized by the large scale of certain companies and by the disproportionality between the financial burden and the benefit obtained by the crime. In this sense, it is only worth mentioning that recidivism on the part of large companies has been perceived with some frequency, which may require a certain practical improvement of the deterrent character for large corporations.

In the British scenario, unlimited fines, as well as other sanctions such as the suspension of operations and the implementation of compliance programs, are designed to act as a deterrent, discouraging not only the company in question, but also other entities in the sector.

This function of punishment has proved to be compatible with the practice of the United Kingdom legal system, where the application of these measures is done in a systematic and judicious manner. The British regulatory framework, supported by a robust judicial system, ensures that sanctions are effectively enforced, ensuring that deterrence is not only theoretical, but concretely achievable.

Finally, in Portugal, the theory of negative general prevention is applied in the context of the criminal liability of business entities to ensure that the application of penalties has an intimidatory and deterrent effect. The Portuguese penal system uses the threat of sanctions to prevent the commission of crimes, seeking to create an environment where compliance with legal norms is encouraged by the fear of severe consequences.

However, it is observed that there is a practical incompatibility in the application of this function of punishment in the Portuguese scenario, since punishments are strictly limited to the degree of guilt of the agent, which weakens the intended deterrent capacity. The deterrent function is compromised when the sanctions imposed are directly proportional to individual guilt, without considering the broader impact that the penalty should have on the collectivity, not generating the necessary intimidating effect to discourage the practice of crimes by other entities.

Another purpose of the sentence that deserves to be highlighted is the rehabilitation function, related to the theory of special positive prevention, which, in Brazil, as it has been explored, differs from other jurisdictions. There is the option that companies, when being criminally convicted, comply with punishments that seek not only punishment, but also social reintegration and the benefit of the community. The provision of services to the community reflects the resocializing and reparative function of the sentence, going beyond the simple retribution for the crime committed.

In the United States, the rehabilitation function is concretized in the imposition of compliance and external supervision programs, aiming to rehabilitate corporations, ensuring that they adopt more ethical practices, reducing recidivism. Thus, the combination of these penalties aims both to repair the damage caused and to transform companies into responsible agents in society.

At the UK level, the rehabilitation function is well established for individuals, but is less emphasized for legal entities, given that the sanctions often imposed are of a financial nature, such as fines, and corrective measures such as publicity orders are rare. Thus, despite the theoretical provision of this purpose, it has no practical support.

Furthermore, in Portugal, the applicable penalties, such as interdictions and prohibitions, do not have a direct impact on the internal rehabilitation of the company, unlike the punishments directed at individuals. The emphasis on measures such as the publicity of the sentence and the prohibition of activities can cause damage to the image of society, but it does not necessarily promote a significant internal structural change. Thus, the effective rehabilitation of legal entities can be limited by the lack of sanctions that stimulate a real transformation in the organization.

Briefly analyzing the function of the neutralization penalty, it was concluded that in Brazil, also known as Special Negative Prevention, it seeks to incapacitate the agent who committed a crime, removing him from social life to avoid recidivism. For business entities, this neutralization is achieved through restrictive sanctions, such as the suspension of activities or the temporary prohibition of establishment, which can be compared to the deprivation of liberty for individuals. It is worth mentioning that, based on analyses, it was concluded that there is efficiency in its application by the Brazilian justice system, and does not need improvement.

In the United States, the function of incapacitation is related to the suspension of activities or even the dissolution of the entity, as occurs in cases of violation of antitrust laws. However, despite the legal provision for such neutralization, studies indicate that in practice, the complete neutralization of companies is rare, and is often avoided by agreements that protect the reputation and continuous operation of corporations, harming the aforementioned function.

At the British level, the neutralization of companies as a function of the penalty is not widely practiced, with the exclusion of companies involved in bribery practices in public tenders, provided for by the Bribery Act of 2010. However, this measure is seen more as a financial and reputational penalty than an effective neutralization, as companies can continue to operate in other sectors (Bribery Act, 2010).

Finally, in Portugal, accessory penalties, such as the prohibition of activities or the suspension of subsidies, can be used to restrict the company's operations, aiming to prevent recurrence, but it has little support in the courts.

In conclusion, in both the United Kingdom and Portugal, the neutralization of societies as a function of punishment faces significant limitations. Thus, the neutralization of companies is not yet fully consolidated as an effective punishment mechanism in both countries, thus undermining a practical support for this purpose of punishment.

The function of respect for the law, often associated with the theory of positive general prevention, also plays a role in preventing crimes through intimidation, not by the amount of punishment, but by the certainty of punishment. However, it is worth mentioning that it only applies in Brazil and Portugal.

In the Brazilian scenario, the theory of positive general prevention is based on psychological intimidation, seeking to prevent the practice of crimes through the threat of punishment, highlighting the importance of public trust in criminal justice and social pacification. However, complex crimes, such as environmental crimes, present significant challenges to the effective application of the theory, as the difficulty in identifying and investigating these crimes can compromise the effectiveness of the purpose of the penalty.

In Portugal, the theory of positive general prevention aims to demonstrate the validity of laws and the confirmation of the values protected by society. However, in the face of statistical data, the effectiveness of the theory is limited in practice. This is because, between 2008 and 2018, there was a significant increase in crimes against property and property, suggesting that, despite the application of penalties, the theory has not been completely effective in preventing illicit practices, requiring review and improvement of punitive measures to strengthen the aforementioned function (Directorate-General for Justice Policy, 2018).

That said, when comparing the functions of punishment in the criminal liability of legal entities between Brazil, the United States, the United Kingdom and Portugal, a diversity of approaches is noted, reflecting the legal and cultural peculiarities of each country. In Brazil, due to the maximum limitations of sanctions or the absence of provision for social reintegration norms, many purposes of punishment end up not having a practical applicability. In addition, the lack of inspection or those being late, greatly undermine trust in the law and the confirmation of society's values.

In the United States and the United Kingdom, the sanction function is strongly linked to retribution and deterrence, with severe financial penalties that serve both to punish and to prevent future corporate infractions, emphasizing the deterrent function and the economic weight of sanctions, however, they end up ignoring other equally relevant functions of punishment. Finally, Portugal faces some challenges, due to the lack of transparency in the judgments issued by the courts of convicted business entities, which greatly impairs the analysis of practical application, in addition, it has a deterrent function compromised by limiting punishments to individual guilt, without considering the broader impact that the penalty should have on the community.

Finally, it is worth mentioning that in Brazil, the United States, the United Kingdom and Portugal, the liability of the business entity is allowed without the need for the conviction of the agent. This reflects an approach that allows corporate entities to be convicted of unlawful conduct committed within the scope of their operations, regardless of the criminal liability of the individuals directly involved.

From these considerations, it is concluded that, although the functions of punishment are universally recognized as essential instruments for the maintenance of order and justice, their practical application in the corporate sphere requires constant adaptation to the economic and social realities of each country. Thus, it is possible to punish a society using as a basis the purposes of the penalty provided for individuals. However, the nuances of the crimes committed by large corporations must be observed by adapting the punishments.

In short, although all these countries share the concern with retribution, deterrence, rehabilitation, respect for the laws and neutralization, the way each of them acts is unique, generating different results, which greatly enriches the theme. Thus, the differences in the practical application and focus of each system reveal the complexities involved in the application of the functions of the penalty in the criminal liability of the business entity.

REFERENCES

Amorim, Manoel Carpena. (2000). Responsabilidade Penal da Pessoa Jurídica. Revista da EMERJ, v.3, n.10. p. 31.

Araújo Júnior, João Marcelo de. (1999). SOCIETAS DELINQUERE NON POTEST- Review of comparative legislation and current state of doctrine, in GOMES, Luiz Flávio (Org.), Responsabilidade penal da pessoa jurídica e medidas provisórias e direito penal. São Paulo: Revista dos Tribunais. p. 93.

Barbosa, Márcio José de Aguiar. (2012). Environmental crimes and the problem of criminal imputation of the legal entity. II Conference on Environmental Law. School of Federal Magistracy 1st Region. Brasília: ESMAF. p 270.

BBC News. (2013). Sellafield appeal over £700,000 waste fine. Available at: <https://www.bbc.com/news/uk-england-cumbria-25013336>. Accessed on: 15 Aug. 2024.

Beccaria, Cesare. (2014). On crimes and penalties. 6 ed. Translated by Torrieri Guimarães. São Paulo: Martin Claret. p. 45.

Becker, Gary Stanley. (1974). Crime and Punishment: An Economic Approach. University of Chicago and National Bureau of Economic Research.

Bitencourt, Cezar Roberto. (2003). Criminal Law Treaty. General part. vol. 1. 8. ed. São Paulo: Saraiva.

Bolzani, Isabela. (2023). Americanas: report points to more than R$ 40 billion between fraud and improper entries. Available at: <https://g1.globo.com/economia/noticia/2023/06/13/americanas-relatorio-mostra-que-fraudes-somam-mais-de-r-40-bilhoes-entenda-o-caso.ghtml>. Accessed on: June 25, 2024.

Botelho, Cristina Ossipe Martins. (2004). The Culpability and Punishment of the Legal Entity in Environmental Crimes: The Necessary Review of Criminal Dogmatics. Postgraduate Thesis in Law at the Federal University of Pernambuco. p. 52, 140, 217, 228.

Brazil. (1940). Penal Code: Decree-Law 2.848/1940. Available at: <https://www.planalto.gov.br/ccivil_03/decreto-lei/del2848compilado.htm>. Accessed on: 06 Feb. 2024. p. 3, 4, 6, 10, 22.

Brazil. (1984). Law No. 7,210/1984. Available at: <https://www.planalto.gov.br/ccivil_03/leis/l7210.htm> Accessed on: 01 mar. 2024. p. 1, 24.

Brazil. (1991). Decree 154, of June 26, 1991. Available at: <https://www.planalto.gov.br/ccivil_03/decreto/1990-1994/d0154.htm>. Accessed on: June 25, 2024. p. 3-5.

Brazil. (1998). Federal Law No. 9,605/1998. Available at: <https://www.planalto.gov.br/ccivil_03/leis/l9605.htm#:~:text=LEI%20N%C2%BA%209.605%2C%20DE%2012%20DE%20FEVEREIRO%20DE%201998.&text=Disp%C3%B5e%20sobre%20as%20san%C3%A7%C3%B5es%20penais,ambiente%2C%20e%20d%C3%A1%20outras%20provid%C3%AAncias.>. Accessed on: 06 Feb. 2024. p. 1-4, 9, 11-12.

Brazil. (2002). Civil Code: Law n. 10.406/2002. Available at: <https://www.planalto.gov.br/ccivil_03/leis/2002/l10406compilada.htm>. Accessed on: 06 Feb. 2024. p. 16, 67, 70.

Brazil. (2004). Decree No. 5,015 of March 15, 2004. Available at: <https://www.planalto.gov.br/ccivil_03/_ato2004-2006/2004/decreto/d5015.htm>. Accessed on: June 25, 2024. p. 5.

Brazil. (2006). Decree No. 5,687, of January 31, 2006. Available at: <https://www.planalto.gov.br/ccivil_03/_Ato2004-2006/2006/Decreto/D5687.htm>. Accessed on: June 25, 2024.

Brazil. (2019). Bill No. 2,787/2019. Available at: <https://www25.senado.leg.br/web/atividade/materias/-/materia/137437> Accessed on: 01 mar. 2024. p. 601.

Brazil. (2022). Decree No. 11,129, of July 11, 2022. Available at: <https://www.planalto.gov.br/ccivil_03/_ato2019-2022/2022/decreto/d11129.htm#:~:text=DECRETO%20N%C2%BA%2011.129%2C%20DE%2011%20DE%20JULHO%20DE%202022&text=Regulamenta%20a%20Lei%20n%C2%BA%2012.846,administra%C3%A7%C3%A3o%20p%C3%BAblica%2C%20nacional%20ou%20estrangeira.>. Accessed on: 29 Feb. 2024. p. 14.

Brazil Mineral. (2023). The Largest Companies in the Mineral Sector. Issue 431 Magazine, Brazil Mineral.

Brazil CPI Report. (2019). Report of the Parliamentary Commission of Inquiry into Brumadinho and Other Dams. Available at: <https://www.camara.leg.br/internet/comissoes/cpi/cpibruma/RelatorioFinal.pdf> Accessed on: 01 mar. 2024. p. 239, 620.

Bribery Act. (2010). c. 23. UK.

Brodt, Luís Augusto Sanzo and Meneghin, Guilherme De Sá. (2015). Criminal liability of the legal entity: a comparative study. Revista dos Tribunais, RT VOL. 961.

Bruno, Aníbal. (2009). Criminal law: general part, volume III: penalty and security measure. 5 rev. and current ed. by Raphael Cirigliano Filho. Rio de Janeiro: Forense. p.12.

Busato, Paulo César. (2018). The criminal liability of legal entities in the history of Brazilian positive law. RIL, Brasília, a. 55, n. 218. p. 91.

Busato, Paulo César. (2019). Tres Tesis sobre la responsabilidad penal de personas jurídicas. Valencia. Tirant Lo Blanch. p.88.

Camargo, Antonio Luis Chaves. (2002). System of penalties, legal-criminal dogmatics and criminal policy. São Paulo: Cultural Paulista. p. 205.

Carmoa, Wendal. (2024). Mariana: 8 years later, mining companies are convicted and will have to pay billionaire compensation, Jornal Extra. Available at: <https://www.cartacapital.com.br/sustentabilidade/mariana-8-

anos-depois-mineradoras-sao-condenadas-e-terao-de-pagar-indenizacao-bilionaria/>. Accessed on: 07 Feb. 2024.

Castro Junior, Ubiratan Barroso de. (2023). Exploring the Complex Legal System of the United States: A Detailed Analysis. Available at: <https://www.jusBrazil.com.br/artigos/explorando-o-complexo-sistema-juridico-dos-estados-unidos-uma-analise-detalhada/1927877098#:~:text=Common%20Law%20e%20Precedentes,legais%20ao%20longo%20do%20tempo>. Accessed on: 15 Aug. 2024. p. 2.

Penal Code of Portugal (1995). Decree-Law No. 48/95 - Penal Code of Portugal.

Coelho Araújo, Marina Pinhão. (2017). In: REALE JÚNIOR, Miguel (coord.). Commented penal code. São Paulo: Saraiva. p. 183.

Federal Constitution. (1988). Constitution of the Federative Republic of Brazil of 1988, Brasília, DF: President of the Republic. Available at: <http://www.planalto.gov.br/ccivil_03/constituicao/constituicao.htm>. Accessed on 06 Dec. 2023. p. 4, 112, 136-137.

Palermo Convention. (2004). Decree No. 5,015, of March 12, 2004. Promulgates the United Nations Convention against Transnational Organized Crime.

Vienna Convention. (2009). Decree No. 7,030, of December 14, 2009. Promulgates the Vienna Convention on the Law of Treaties, concluded on May 23, 1969, with reservations to Articles 25 and 66.

Cordeiro, Maria Eugenia Batista. (2023). The Criminal Liability of the Legal Entity in Money Laundering Crimes. Federal University of Rio Grande do Norte. p. 143-152.

Corporate Manslaughter and Corporate Homicide Act. (2007). c. 19. UK.

Criminal Finances Act. (2017). c. 22. UK.

D'Agostino, Rosanne. (2015). Dam rupture in Mariana: questions and answers, G1. Available at: <https://g1.globo.com/ciencia-e-saude/

noticia/2015/11/rompimento-de-barragens-em-mariana-perguntas-e-respostas.html>. Accessed on: 25 jan. 2024. p. 13.

From Filippo, Thiago Baldani Gomes. (2016). Risk society and objective criminal liability: analysis of the crimes of mere imputation of the United States. Empório do Direito. p. 3.

Desidério, Mariana. (2018). Corruption at Odebrecht is the most organized in the history of capitalism. Available at: <https://www.justice.gov/sites/default/files/criminal-fraud/legacy/2012/11/14/fcpa-english.pdf>. Accessed on: June 17, 2024.

Directorate-General for Justice Policy. (2018). Ministry of Justice. Available at: <https://estatisticas.justica.gov.pt/sites/siej/pt-pt>. Accessed on: 15 Aug. 2024.

Dotti, René Ariel. (1995). The criminal incapacity of the legal entity. Brazilian Journal of Criminal Sciences, São Paulo, v. 11. p. 201.

Dotti, René Ariel. (1998). Bases and alternatives for the system of penalties. 2nd ed. São Paulo: Editora Revista dos Tribunais. p. 176, 215.

Dotti, René Ariel. (2010). Criminal liability of the legal entity: in defense of the principle of subjective imputation. 2nd ed. São Paulo: Revista dos Tribunais. p. 422.

Doyle, Charles. (2013). Corporate Criminal Liability: An Overview of Federal Law. Senior Specialist in American Public Law. p. 5.

Elstein, Aaron. (2019). Corporate Crime and Punishment: An Empirical Study. Texas Law Review. Available at: <https://texaslawreview.org/corporate-crime-and-punishment-an-empirical-study/>. Accessed on: 15 Aug. 2024.

Environment Agency. (2017). Thames Water ordered to pay record £20 million for river pollution. Available at: <https://www.gov.uk/government/news/thames-water-ordered-to-pay-record-20-million-for-river-pollution>. Accessed on: 15 Aug. 2024.

United States. Sherman Antitrust Act. Provides for the fight against monopolistic practices and guarantees fair competition in the market, from 1890. Available at: <https://www.archives.gov/milestone-documents/sherman-anti-trust-act>. Accessed on: June 25, 2024.

United States. Foreign Corrupt Practices Act. Provides for the Law of Corrupt Practices Abroad, of 1977. Available at: <https://www.justice.gov/sites/default/files/criminal-fraud/legacy/2012/11/14/fcpa-english.pdf>. Accessed on: June 25, 2024.

Ferguson, Gerry. (2019). Corruption And Corporate Criminal Liability. Available at: <https://icclr.org/wp-content/uploads/2019/06/FergusonG.pdf?x21689#:~:text=The%20identification%20doctrine%20holds%20corporations,as%20occurs%20under%20vicarious%20liability>. Accessed on: 15 Aug. 2024.

Feuerbach, Anselm von Ritter. (1989). Tratado de Derecho Penal. Trad. Eugenio Raul Zaffaroni and Irma Hagemeier. Buenos Aires: Hammurabi. p. 57-64.

Figueiredo Dias, Jorge de. (1998). Brief considerations on the foundation, meaning and application of penalties in economic criminal law. In Economic and European Criminal Law: Doctrinal Texts. Vol I. Coimbra Editora.

FATF. (2012). Financial Action Task Force. International Standards for Combating Money Laundering and the Financing of Terrorism and Proliferation. The FATF Recommendations. Available at: <https://www.fatf-gafi.org/content/dam/fatf-gafi/translations/Recommendations/FATF-40-Rec-2012-Portuguese-GAFISUD.pdf.coredownload.inline.pdf>. Accessed in: 06/25/2024. p. 14.

Galvão, Fernando. (2003). Responsabilidade penal da pessoa jurídica. 2. ed. Belo Horizonte: Del Rey.

Garrett, Brandon. (2016). The Rise of Bank Prosecutions, 126. YALE L.J.F. p. 33, 40, 63. 125.

Gierke, Otto von. (1934). Natural law and the theory of society. Trad. by Ernest Barker. Vol. I. London: Cambridge Universty Press.

Gomes, Luiz Flávio. (1999). Responsabilidade penal da pessoa jurídica e medidas provisórias e direito penal. São Paulo: Revista dos Tribunais. p. 94.

Gonçalves, Heliana; Batista, Roberta. (2023). Understand the impacts on the Mundaú lagoon in the event of a collapse of the Braskem mine in Maceió, G1. Available at: <https://g1.globo.com/al/alagoas/noticia/2023/12/10/entenda-os-impactos-na-lagoa-mundau-em-caso-de-colapso-da-mina-da-braskem-em-maceio.ghtml>. Accessed on: 05 Feb. 2024, p. 3-7.

Greco, Rogério. Criminal Law Course. 8th ed. Rio de Janeiro: Impetus, 2007. p. 173.

Grotius, Hugo. (2005). The Law of War and Peace. 2. ed. Ijuí: Unijuí. v. 2.

Guaragni, Fábio André; LOUREIRO, Maria Fernanda. (2012). Law 9605/98 and the model of imputation of crime to the legal entity: case studies. Criminal Law and Criminology. XXI CONPEDI Publication. Florianópolis: Editora FUNJAB. p. 136-137.

Hassemer, Winfried. (2007). Libertarian criminal law. Belo Horizonte: Del Rey. p. 82.

Hassemer, Masson, Cleber. (2011). Direito Penal, vol. 1. São Paulo: Método. p. 543.

Hegel, Georg Wilhelm Friedrich. (2009). Principles of Philosophy of Law. 1st ed, 4th edition. São Paulo: Martins Fontes.

Júnior, Odilon. (2019). Criminal Liability of the Legal Entity of Private Law: Money Laundering Crimes. Available at: <https://www.jusBrazil.com.br/artigos/responsabilidade-penal-da-pessoa-juridica-de-direito-privado-crimes-de-lavagem-de-dinheiro/798490633>. Accessed on: 06 set. 2024. p. 36.

Júnior, Vicente de Paula Maciel and Gomes, Reginaldo Gonçalves. (2022). Criminal liability of the legal entity in the Brazilian legal system. Journal of the Undergraduate Course in Law at Unijuí. p. 13.

Law Commission. (2021). Corporate Criminal Liability: A discussion paper. p. 16.

Lecey, Eladio. (1999). The protection of the environment and the criminal liability of the legal entity. In Journal of the Association of Judges of Rio Grande do Sul, Porto Alegre: AJURIS. p. 171.

Law 9.613. (1998). Provides for the crimes of "laundering" or concealment of assets, rights and values. Presidency of the Republic Civil House. p. 3, 5.

Leite, André Lamas. (2020). Political-criminal foundations of the criminal liability of legal persons in classical Criminal Law, applicable substitute penalties and compliance. Revista do Ministério Público 161. p. 218-219.

Lund, Dorothy S.; SARIN, Natasha. (2021). Corporate Crime and Punishment: An Empirical Study. Texas Law Review. Columbia Law School. Scholarship Archive. p. 338-339.

Mansur, Rafaela. (2023). Four years since the tragedy in Brumadinho: 270 deaths, three missing and no punishment, G1. Available at: <https://g1.globo.com/mg/minas-gerais/noticia/2023/01/25/quatro-anos-da-tragedia-em-brumadinho-270-mortes-tres-desaparecidos-e-nenhuma-punicao.ghtml>. Accessed on: 25 jan. 2024.

Markoff, G. (2013). Arthur Andersen and the Myth of the Corporate Death Penalty: Corporate Criminal Convictions in the Twenty-First Century. University of Pennsylvania Journal of Business Law. p. 15.

Martins, José Fernando. (2023). Sale of Braskem may exempt new owners from paying for the mining company's crimes, Jornal Extra. Available at: <https://ojornalextra.com.br/noticias/alagoas/2023/12/99035-venda-da-braskem-pode-isentar-novos-donos-de-pagar-pelos-crimes-da-mineradora>. Accessed on: 25 jan. 2024. p. 3

Martins, Lourenço. (2011). The Measure of Punishment - Purposes and Choice. Critical Approach to Doctrine and Jurisprudence. Coimbra Editora.

Marques, Oswaldo Henrique Duek. (1998). The liability of the legal entity for offense to the environment. Boletim IBCCrim., São Paulo, n. 65, p. 7.

Mendonça, Alberico. (2007). The FATF/FATF Recommendations: soft or hard law? Journal of the Master's Degree in Law, Brasília: Catholic University of Brazilia, v. 1, n. 1. Available at: <https://portalrevistas.ucb.br/index.php/rvmd/article/viewFile/2618/1608>. Accessed on: 15 Aug. 2024.

Mendonça, Heloísa. (2021). Vale signs an agreement to pay 37.68 billion reais in reparation for the tragedy in Brumadinho, El País. Available at: <https://Brazil.elpais.com/Brazil/2021-02-04/vale-assina-acordo-para-pagar-3768-bilhoes-de-reais-de-reparacao-por-tragedia-de-brumadinho.html>. Accessed on: 08 Feb. 2024.

Ministry of Justice. (2020). Criminal Justice system statistics quarterly. Table Q5.1.

Mirabete, Julio Fabbrini. Manual de direito penal. 21 ed. São Paulo: Atlas, 2004. p. 122.

Mourullo, Gonzalo Rodríguez. (1978). Derecho Penal: Parte General. Madrid: Editorial Civitas. p. 227-228.

MPMG. (2020). MPMG and PCMG conclude investigations into the dam collapse in Brumadinho: 16 people are charged with aggravated homicide and environmental crimes. Available at: <https://www.mpmg.mp.br/portal/menu/comunicacao/noticias/mpmg-e-pcmg-finalizam-investigacoes-sobre-o-rompimento-da-barragem-em-brumadinho-16-pessoas-sao-denunciadas-por-homicidio-qualificado-e-crimes-ambientais.shtml>. Accessed on: 15 Feb. 2024.

Nascimento, Pablo. (2023). Samarco dam rupture completes 8 years with defendants free of homicide complaints, R7. Available at: <https://noticias.r7.com/minas-gerais/rompimento-de-barragem-da-samarco-completa-8-anos-com-reus-livres-de-denuncia-de-homicidios-04112023>. Accessed on: 07 Feb. 2024.

Nery, Déa Carla Pereira. (2005). Theories of Punishment and its Purpose in Brazilian Criminal Law, Legal Universe, Juiz de Fora. Available at: <https://

egov.ufsc.br/portal/conteudo/teorias-da-pena-e-sua-finalidade-no-direito-penal-Brazileiro>. Accessed on: 26 Feb. 2024.

Netto, Alamiro Velludo Salvador. (2018). Criminal liability of the legal entity. São Paulo: RT. p. 266.

New York Central & Hudson River Railroad Co. V. United States. (1909). 212 U.S. p. 481, 494-495.

Noronha, Magalhães. (1988). Direito Penal, Vol. I. São Paulo: Saraiva. p. 110.

OECD. (2016). OECD Convention Against Transnational Bribery. Ministry of Transparency, Inspection and Control. p. 11.

Palma, Maria Fernanda. (2016). Criminal Law. Material concept of crime, principles and foundations. Principle of legality: interpretation of the criminal law and application of the criminal law in time. AAFDL Editora. p. 57.

Pereira, Ana Sofia Rodrigues. (2018). The purpose of the penalty of the legal person in the Portuguese Penal Code. Faculty of Law of the University of Coimbra. p. 53, 58.

Prado, Luiz Regis. (2013). Brazilian criminal law course. 12. ed. São Paulo: Revista dos Tribunais, p. 544.

Puig, Santiago Mir. (2007). Criminal law: foundations and theory of crime. São Paulo: Revista dos Tribunais. p. 64-65, 68.

Reale Júnior, Miguel. (2001). The criminal liability of the business entity. In: PRADO, Luiz Regis (Coord.). Criminal liability of the business entity: in defense of the principle of subjective criminal imputation. São Paulo: R. dos Tribunais. p. 137-139.

Reid, Vanessa. (2023). Key Changes to Corporate Liability in the Economic Crime and Corporate Transparency Act 2023 – Expanded Identification Doctrine and New Failure to Prevent Fraud Offence. The Economic Crime and Corporate Transparency Act 2023 introduces several significant changes to criminal liability for organizations, although the ultimate impact of the Act on corporate crime remains to be seen. Available at: <https://www.mountfordchambers.com/key-changes-to-corporate-liability-in-the-economic-crime-and-corporate-transparency-act-2023-expanded-identification-doctrine-and-new-failure-to-prevent-fraud-offence/>. Accessed on: 15 Aug. 2024. p. 3.

Reform Of Offences Against The Person. (2015) Law Com No. 361, 2.3.

Ribeiro, Bruno de Moraes. (2008). The function of social reintegration of the deprivation of liberty sentence. Porto Alegre: Sergio Antonio Fabris Ed.

Rocha, Fernando A. N. Galvão da. (1998). Responsabilidade penal da pessoa jurídica. In Journal of Environmental Law. São Paulo: Revista dos Tribunais.

Roper, Victoria Elizabeth. (2016). EXPERT COMMENT: UK corporate manslaughter cases tend to be complex and can take years to reach a finding. The Conversation. Available at: <https://www.northumbria.ac.uk/about-us/news-events/news/expert-comment-lucy-letby-investigation-uk-corporate-manslaughter-cases-tend-to-be-complex-and-can-take-years-to-reach-a-finding/#:~:text=The%20main%20penalty%20for%20corporate,more%20than%20%C2%A31%20million>. Accessed on: 15 Aug. 2024.

Rosenthal, Lee H. (2009). United States v. BP Products North America Inc. Casetext. Available at: <https://casetext.com/case/us-v-bp-products-north-america-inc-3>. Accessed on: 15 Aug. 2024.

Roxin, Claus. (1976). Sentidos y limites de la pena estatal. In: Problemas básicos del derecho penal, {Sentidos e limites da pena estatal. In: Basic Problems of Criminal Law}, Translation and Notes by Diego- Manuel Luzon Peña. Madrid: REUS S.A. p. 15.

Roxin, Claus. (1997). Derecho Penal: parte general, {Direito Penal: parte geral}, Trans. Diego Manuel Luzon Peña et. al. Madrid: Civitas. p. 91-92.

Roxin, Claus. (2013). The protection of legal assets as a function of criminal law, Org. and trans. André Luís Callegari and Nereu José Giacomolli, 2nd ed. Porto Alegre: Livraria do Advogado Editora. p. 27.

R. V. Balfour Beatty Rail Infrastructure Services LTD. (2006). EWCA Crim 1586. 1 All ER 191.

R. V. Cotswold Geotechnical Holdings LTD. (2011). EWCA Crim 1337. 1 WLR 2275.

R. V. Huggins And Barnes. (1730). 94 ER 708.

Sá, Sidnei Boccia Pinto De Oliveira. (2006). Rethinking the retributive function of criminal punishment. De jure: legal journal of the Public Prosecutor's Office of the State of Minas Gerais.

Sales, Sheila Jorge Selim de. (1993). Do Subject Ativo na Parte Especial do Código Penal. Belo Horizonte: Livraria Del Rey Editora. p. 29.

Santos, Juarez Cirino dos. (2010). Criminal liability of the legal entity In: PRADO, Luiz Regis; DOTTI, René Ariel (Coord.) Criminal liability of the legal entity: in defense of the principle of subjective imputation, 2nd ed. São Paulo: Revista dos Tribunais. p. 281.

Savigny, Friedrich Karl von. (1879). Sistema del derecho romano actual, Tomo II Trad. de M. CH. Guenoux. Madrid: F. Góngora.

Sentencing Code. (2020). c. 17. UK.

Serious Fraud Office V Barclays. (2018). PLC. EWHC. 3055. QB.

Shecaira, Sérgio Salomão. (1998). Responsabilidade penal da pessoa jurídica. São Paulo: Revista dos Tribunais. p. 86, 88.

Shecaira, Sérgio Salomão. (2013). Responsabilidade penal da pessoa jurídica. São Paulo: Método. 2003 In II ESMAF Environmental Law Conference. TRF1st. Brazilia.

Sherman Antitrust Act. (1890). 15 U.S.C. §§ 1-7. Sherman Antitrust Act.

Silva, Germano Marques da. (2008). The Theory of Penalties and Security Measures, 2nd Ed. Editorial Verbo. p. 34.

Silva, Sávio Renato Bittencourt. (2002). The criminal liability of the legal entity: a new theory of culpability, In Revista do Ministério Público. Rio de Janeiro: Ministério Público. p. 178.

Silveira, Rafael Pelizzaro da. (2017). Criminal Liability of the Busness Entity. A perspective from the perspective of the theory of crime. Federal University of Uberlândia. p. 117-118, 126.

Smanio, Gianpaolo Poggio. (2000). Criminal protection of diffuse interests. São Paulo: Atlas.

Souza, José Carlos Rodrigues de. (1988). Responsabilidade penal da pessoa jurídica e sua justificativa social, In Revista de Direito Ambiental. São Paulo: Revista dos Tribunais. p. 140.

Supreme Court of Justice. (2005). Special Appeal No. 564.960 - SC (2003/0107368-4). Rapporteur: Justice Gilson Dipp. APPELLANT: PUBLIC PROSECUTOR'S OFFICE OF THE STATE OF SANTA CATARINA. Defendant: Auto Posto 1270 Ltda - Microenterprise. Brasília (DF), June 2, 2005 (Date of Judgment). Fifth Panel of the Supreme Court of Justice. Available at: <https://www.stj.jus.br/websecstj/cgi/revista/REJ.cgi/ATC?seq=1791222&tipo=0&nreg=&SeqCgrmaSessao=&CodOrgaoJgdr=&dt=&formato=PDF&salvar=false>. Accessed on: 03 set. 2024.

Supreme Court of Justice. (2015). Appeal in Writ of Mandamus No. 39.173 - BA. p. 13.

Supreme Court of Justice: Sixth Panel. (2018). Regimental Appeal in the Special Appeal. STJ - AGRG NO RESP 1712991 / SP 2017/0313343-9. Judging Body: Sixth Panel. Rapporteur: Justice Nefi Cordeiro. p. 1.

Federal Supreme Court. (1988). Appeal in Habeas Corpus. RHC 66.102/SP, 1st Panel, Rel. Min. Moreira Alves, DJ 05/03/1988.

Federal Supreme Court. (2004). Habeas Corpus. HC 83.301/RS, 1st Panel, Rel. Min. César Peluso, DJ 03.16.2004.

Federal Supreme Court. (2005). Ordinary Constitutional Appeal (RHC) 85.658/ES. Rapporteur: Minister Cezar Peluso. 1st Panel of the STF. June 21, 2005.

Federal Supreme Court. (2005). HC 83554 PR. Rapporteur: Justice Gilmar Mendes. DJ 28-10-2005 PP-00060 EMENT VOL-02211-01 PP-00155 LEXSTF v. 27, n. 324, 2005. August 16, 2005. Second Panel. Available at: <https://www.jusBrazil.com.br/jurisprudencia/stf/763658>. Accessed on: 03 set. 2024. p. 368-383.

Federal Supreme Court. (2008). HC 92.921-4/BA. Rapporteur: Justice Ricardo Lewandowski. DJe-182 DIVULG 25-09-2008 PUBLIC 26-09-2008 EMENT VOL-02334-03 PP-00439 RJSP v. 56, n. 372, 2008. August 18, 2008. 1st Panel of the STF. Available at: <https://www.jusBrazil.com.br/jurisprudencia/stf/14719240>. Accessed on: 03 set. 2024. p. 167-185.

Federal Supreme Court. (2011). AgRg in RE 628.582/RS. Rapporteur: Justice Dias Toffoli. DJe-042 DIVULG 02/03/2011 PUBLIC 03/03/2011. September 6, 2011. 1st Panel. Available at: <https://www.jusBrazil.com.br/jurisprudencia/stf/18314052>. Accessed on: 03 set. 2024.

Federal Supreme Court. (2013). Extraordinary Appeal 548.181 Paraná. Rapporteur: Justice Rosa Weber. First Panel.

Tesco V Nattrass. (1972). AC 153. 2 WLR 1166. 2 All ER. p. 127.

The FATF Recommendations. (2023). International Standards On Combating Money Laundering And The Financing Of Terrorism & Proliferation. p. 39.

TRF-1st, 4th Panel. (2012). AP 2003.39.00.014345-3/PA. Rel. Des. Fed. Mário César Ribeiro, on 04/24/2012.

TRF-4. (2019). Criminal Appeal: ACR 50013165820184047121. RS 5001316-58.2018.4.04.712. 28/02/2019.

Court of Appeal of Coimbra. (2015). Case: 194/13.5IDLRA. C1. Judgment of the Court of Appeal of Coimbra of 04/02/2015. Rapporteur: Vasques Osório. Descriptors: Sentence measurement. PENALTY OF FINE.

Daily rate. INSUFFICIENCY FOR THE DECISION OF THE PROVEN FACTS. Date of the Judgment: 02/04/2015. Available at: <https://www.dgsi.pt/JTRC.NSF/c3fb530030ea1c61802568d9005cd5bb/0cd4d14921b2c3da80257de80050e253?OpenDocument>. Accessed on: 15 Aug. 2024.

Court of Appeal of Coimbra. (2022). Case: 82/20.9GEACB-A. C1. Judgment of the Court of Appeal of Coimbra of 02/02/2022. Rapporteur: João Novais. Keywords: Violation of safety rules. Blank Penalties Norms. Principle of legality. Principle of typicality. Penalties applicable to business entities. Date of the Judgment: 02/02/2022. Available at: <https://www.dgsi.pt/jtrc.nsf/8fe0e606d8f56b22802576c0005637dc/ffc4728de4f274d8802587e3003d8877?OpenDocument>. Accessed on: 15 Aug. 2024.

Court of Appeal of Évora. (2012). Case: 60/09.9TAVVC. E1. Judgment of the Court of Appeal of Évora of 26-06-2012. Rapporteur: Ana Barata Brito. Keywords: Abuse of Trust Against Social Security. Criminal Liability of the Business Entity. Date of the Judgment: 06/26/2012. Available at: <https://www.dgsi.pt/jtre.nsf/134973db04f39bf2802579bf005f080b/32df9e916845e4a480257de10056f889?OpenDocument>. Accessed on: 15 Aug. 2024.

Court of Appeal of Évora. (2016). Case: 1966/13.6TAPTM. E1. Judgment of the Court of Appeal of Évora of 10/05/2016. Rapporteur: João Amaro. Keywords: Qualified Fraud. Document forgery. Business Entity. Date of the Judgment: 05/10/2016. Available at: <https://www.dgsi.pt/jtre.nsf/-/0A95E647DBB7414280257FCB004EBBE2>. Accessed on: 15 Aug. 2024.

Lisbon Court of Appeal. (2021). Case: 1104/17.6Y5LSB. L1-5. Judgment of the Lisbon Court of Appeal of 21/12/2021. Rapporteur: Paulo Barreto. Keywords: Administrative Offence Appeal. Liability of the Business Entity. Date of the Judgment: 12/21/2021. Available at: <https://diariodarepublica.pt/dr/detalhe/acordao/1104-2021-189995175>. Accessed on: 15 Aug. 2024.

Lisbon Court of Appeal. (2021). Case: 1874/19.7T8TVD. L1-5. Judgment of the Lisbon Court of Appeal of 12/01/2021. Rapporteur: Vieira Lamim. Keywords: Administrative Offence Appeal. Challenge of the Facts. Liability of the Business Entity. Date of the Judgment: 01/12/2021. Available at: <https://

diariodarepublica.pt/dr/detalhe/acordao/1874-2021-190111075>. Accessed on: 15 Aug. 2024.

Lisbon Court of Appeal. (2023). Case: 940/20.0T9FNC. L1-5. Judgment of the Lisbon Court of Appeal of 13/07/2023. Rapporteur: Mafalda Sequinho dos Santos. Descriptors: Economic Crimes. Criminal Liability of the Business Entity. Date of the Judgment: 07/13/2023. Available at: <https://www.dgsi.pt/jtrl.nsf/33182fc732316039802565fa00497eec/5103edd3f6dfc80180258a220044774c?OpenDocument>. Accessed on: 15 Aug. 2024.

Tristão, Adalto Dias. (1999). Criminal Sentence, 4th ed. Belo Horizonte: Del Rey.

United States Sentencing Commission. (2023). Guidelines Manual. U.S. Sentencing Guidelines.

United States V. A&P Trucking CO. (1958). 358 U.S. p. 121, 123.

United States V. Armstrong. (1996). 517 U.S. p. 456, 464.

United States v. Hougland Barge Line, INC. (1974). 387 F. Supp. W.D.Pa. 1974. p. 1110, 1114.

United States V. Jorgensen. (1998). 144 F.3d. 8th Cir. 1998. p. 550, 560.

United States v. Jpmorgan Chase & CO. (2014). Settlement Agreement, No. 14-CV-00197.

United States V. Nixon. (1974). 418 U.S. p. 683, 693.

United States V. Park. (1975). 421 U.S. p. 658.

United States V. Polizzi. (1974). 500 f.2d. 9th Cir. 1974. p. 856, 907.

United States V. Potter. (2006). 463 F.3d 9. 1st Cir. 2006. p. 25.

United States V. Sun Diamond Growers. (1998). 138 F.3d. D.C.Cir. 1998. p. 961.

United States V. Volkswagen AG. (2017). No. 16-CR-20394. WL 119093.

U.S. (1789). Eighth Amendment to the United States Constitution.

U.S. Code. (2023). 18 U.S.C. § 3553(a).

U.S. Department of Justice. (2015). BNP Paribas Sentenced for Conspiring to Violate the International Emergency Economic Powers Act and the Trading with the Enemy Act. Available at: <https://www.justice.gov/opa/pr/bnp-paribas-sentenced-conspiring-violate-international-emergency-economic-powers-act-and>. Accessed on: 15 Aug. 2024.

Vareilles-Sommieres, Marquis de. (1919). Les personnes morales. Paris: Livrarie Générale de Droit et de Jurisprudence F. Pichon et Durand-Auzias.

Wall Street Journal. (2014). France Claims Victory in BNP Paribas Case. French Authorities Lobbied U.S. for Months Over Settlement. Available at: <https://www.wsj.com/articles/france-claims-victory-in-bnp-paribas-case-1404211120>. Accessed on: 15 Aug. 2024.

Wayte V. United States. (1985). 470 U.S. p. 598, 607.

Welzel, Hans. (1993). Derecho Penal Alemán: Parte General, 11th German ed., 4th ed. Castellana, {German Criminal Law: General Part, 11th German edition, 4th edition in Spanish}, Trans. Juan Bustos Ramirez. Santiago: Valparaíso. p.13.

Zaffaroni, Eugênio Raul. (1996) Manual de Derecho Penal – Parte General. Buenos Aires: Editora Ediar. p. 339.

Zaffaroni, Eugenio Raúl. (1997). Manual de Direito Penal Brazileiro, Volume 1 - General Part. p. 390.

Zuba, Fernando; FREITAS, Raquel. (2023). Brumadinho: Two days before the statute of limitations for environmental crimes, MPF offers a complaint to the Federal Court, G1. Available at: <https://g1.globo.com/mg/minas-gerais/noticia/2023/01/23/brumadinho-ha-dois-dias-do-prazo-para-prescricao-de-crimes-ambientais-mpf-oferece-denuncia-a-justica-federal.ghtml>. Accessed on: 25 jan. 2024.

Made in the USA
Monee, IL
04 November 2026

67377513R00105